More Praise

"Febos's own voice is so irreverent and ... is not simply to tell about her own li... ... pulses of many others'." —*The New York Times Book Review*

"The harrowing nature of . . . transformation is *Girlhood*'s core subject, and in seven chapters Febos explores the interconnected aspects of patriarchy and the marks that they've left on her . . . Magisterial." —*The New Yorker*

"Febos is an intoxicating writer, but I found myself most grateful for the vivid clarity of her thinking . . . Disquisitive and catalytic—it doesn't demand change so much as expose certain injustices so starkly that you might feel you cannot abide them another minute . . . I never once needed trigonometry and I couldn't find Catullus in a crossword these days, but Febos's education is a kind I surely could have used." —*The Atlantic*

"By following Febos's distinct paths between the past and present, we might realize there's room to forge our own, and that we've just been handed a flashlight that helps illuminate the way." —NPR.org

"I wish I could have read *Girlhood* when I was young . . . Over the course of eight essays with poignant illustrations by Forsyth Harmon . . . Febos illuminates how women are conditioned to be complicit in our own exploitation. Like much of her scholarship, it begins with somatic knowledge of the self." —*The Washington Post*

"Intellectual and erotic, engaging and empowering, [*Girlhood*] offers us exquisite, ferocious language for embracing self-pleasure and self-love." —*Oprah Daily*, "LGBTQ Books That Will Change the Literary Landscape"

"Haunting . . . In sharing the darkness that clouded her coming of age, Febos asks pointed questions about the expectations placed on women and how they impact a person's sense of self." —*Time*

"A dazzling cartography of the violence, shame, and control visited on young women, at the expense of their happiness and freedom. Febos charts a liberating way forward in this galvanizing book, clearing a path for women to feel rage, power, and pleasure." —*Esquire*

"Febos is a precise, visceral chronicler of what it means to be a woman . . . [*Girlhood*] is fierce and lyrical, furious and tender; a vital read for anyone figuring out who they really are, and have always been." —Refinery29

"Febos' latest book is a memoir, but it also serves as a history lesson. [Its] lyrical, meditative writing makes it all the easier to ponder her critical questions and explorations." —*San Francisco Chronicle*

"Searing and poignant, inviting complexity and allowing room for the bevy of emotions women have been conditioned to suppress . . . Required reading." —*The Millions*

"Reimagines what it means to be female in a world hostile to your survival." —*BookPage*

"Disrupt[s] the normative narratives surrounding girlhood and encourages us to recreate ourselves according to ourselves." —*Ms.*

"What a delight it is to read the new book of a writer you adore and be knocked out all over again. With *Girlhood*, one of the queer community's favorite writers, Melissa Febos, has written her career-best." —*The Advocate*

"Febos is a balletic memoirist whose capacious gaze can take in so many seemingly disparate things and unfurl them in a graceful, cohesive way . . . [She] dances deftly between her own autobiography and exposing the pervasive social history that marked—sometimes literally—her personal experiences and those of many, many women." —*Oprah Daily*

"Vibrant, haunting, and absolutely unforgettable . . . A modern masterpiece of brutally honest self-reflection." —*Bust*

"Febos is widely considered one of the most respected and beloved contemporary essayists and memoirists, and a pillar of thought and encouragement for other writers. The essays in her latest collection read like sculpture: sentences chiseled and combined into profound, moving works . . . Philosophical, humorous, and sensual." —*BOMB*

"In each of *Girlhood*'s essays—which are accompanied by gorgeous illustrations by artist/author Forsyth Harmon—Febos works to interrogate her own behaviors as she navigates relationships, love, sex, and addiction and, bolstered by research and interviews, comes out the other side with a clearer understanding of what it might take to make girlhood a less-destructive experience." —Shondaland

"Showcases [Febos'] trademark lyrical range. As a woman, it's impossible not to relate to Febos' essays, and the way she concludes many of them models how we might reframe our experiences as well." —*The Boston Globe*

"Affirms that our shared attitudes and beliefs about girls and the women we expect them to become are more important than whatever benefits we gain by denying and distorting them. *Girlhood* offers the plausibility that on the other side of personal and collective awareness lies the choice to play a different game." —*Chicago Review of Books*

"Febos' blend of reportage and memoir come together for a feminist statement of stunning insight." —The A.V. Club

"Profoundly wise and healing, fearless and generous at once. With *Girlhood*, Febos has become much more than the edgy-but-brainy literary wild-child *Whip Smart* announced her as a decade ago, but rather—still only in her early 40s—one of our most crucial American writers." —*Los Angeles Review of Books*

"Melissa Febos brilliantly explores society's definition of becoming a woman and the values—or lack thereof—it taught her growing up." —*Marie Claire*

"Intimate, poetic, and revelatory . . . *Girlhood* does what an essay collection should do at its best: offer the reader a companion, fellowship beyond the aspirational profit economy models of self-care." —*Electric Literature*

"Forces us to linger in the nuances of sexuality, gender, consent, and eroticism . . . If there is a way out, it might be through books like this one that give us a shared language for all the murky things we as women feel—but too rarely speak." —PopSugar

"How do you heal from the pain of growing up? This question, refracted through a feminist lens, lies at the heart of Melissa Febos's essay collection, *Girlhood*. With psychological clarity and emotional precision, Febos revisits the past to rewrite the future." —*Columbia Journal*

"A landmark book . . . An invitation to collective soul-searching, beyond rage and retribution. Febos's voice is that of righteous anger tempered by cool, patient analysis and compassion. It is just the voice we need." —*The Rumpus*

"An exposé and a corrective, a memoir and a polemic. [Febos] once again turns her keen intellect and unflinching honesty toward myriad personal stories that have wider implications for girls' and women's narratives . . . *Girlhood* is a book that deserves to be savored, to be read more than once, to be given to all the people in your life." —*Washington Independent Review of Books*

"Febos's writing is always luminous, fearless, and blazing with intelligence."
—*LitHub*, "Most Anticipated Books of 2021"

"Dazzling . . . Captures the potency of a woman's adolescence—an experience that is at once singular and universal, familiar and uncharted, ordinary and remarkable. By plumbing the depths of her own coming-of-age, interviewing other women about their early sexual encounters, and interrogating depictions of female sexuality in literature and film, the author unravels the stories women learn to tell—and believe—about themselves." —*Guernica*

"Through lush, pleasurably painful essays [Febos's memoir], written like a retrospective, functions as an anti-coming-of-age story. It's a raw, intimate elegy for an innocence that was never hers to begin with and a recovery of the self, both divine and corporeal." —*Bitch*

"Intimate, beautiful, honest, *Girlhood* is a must read for women who desire modes of resilience and reclamation in thought." —*Columbia Journal of Literary Criticism*

"Never before have I read an essay collection that captures exactly the feeling of a sleepover with my best friend, whispering to each other in the dark."
—*The Brooklyn Rail*

"A manifesto of all the ways girlhood takes a toll on a girl's life . . . Febos's writing shocks and stings: her essays—rife with research, interviews, and other sources—mirror my own experience, my friends' experiences, experiences my mother has told me about . . . What Febos examines in *Girlhood*, in other words, is everywhere." —*Ploughshares*

"Gives us permission to feel anger, grief, power, and pleasure when society constantly denies our experiences." —*Real Simple*

"Already an accomplished memoirist, Febos pauses to take a wider look at the social and cultural forces that shifted her self-perception and possession as her body changed at age eleven . . . She frees herself from patriarchal tropes in the hopes of also freeing others." —*Observer*

"Expand[s] the lexicons of the female experience and the queer experience . . . These essays are safe spaces, full of both darkness and joy and, most notably, the acute relief that comes from seeing yourself in someone else's art." —*The Coachella Review*

"We were clearly overdue for a leftist, queer, feminist analysis of girlhood in 2021, and Melissa Febos has given it to us." —*The Nation*

"Lush with bodily experiences, cultural analysis, media criticism, and classical myth . . . *Girlhood* will leave you breathless and raw, feeling both that a chasm has been opened in your chest and that a hand has been extended to pull you out." —*Fools Magazine*

"This is the book I will buy for all the women I love . . . Febos's smart, intimate, and gorgeous *Girlhood* enlivens the spirit." —*Aster(ix) Journal*

"Phenomenal . . . [Febos shows] how one event or relationship can influence others, and how the unrelenting grip of the patriarchy affects us all." —Newcity Lit

"Lucidly articulates the infuriating and redemptive ways women's lives are shaped . . . Illuminating." —*Shelf Awareness* (starred review)

"Profound and gloriously provocative, this book—a perfect follow-up to her equally visceral previous memoir, *Abandon Me*—transforms the wounds and scars of lived female experience into an occasion for self-understanding that is both honest and lyrical. Consistently illuminating, unabashedly ferocious writing." —*Kirkus Reviews* (starred review)

"In this book of liberating inquiry and divine depth, Febos again and again connects the constellations of herself and the world she and all women must learn to live in." —*Booklist* (starred review)

"Raw and unflinching, this dark coming-of-age story impresses at every turn." —*Publisher's Weekly*

"Powerful, raw, and provocative . . . The author's critique of becoming is as tender as it is relentless . . . A thought-provoking collection that will appeal to fans of fierce feminist prose." —*Library Journal*

"I read *Girlhood* in a long, marvelous guzzle and plan to teach it. Its language and emotional candor deepen the conversation on sexuality and the horrible liberties taken when we're way too young to consent. But there's not an ounce of victim in Melissa Febos and she's a hero without ever trying to be. A classic!" —Mary Karr

"These essays are moss and iron—hard and beautiful—and struck through with Febos' signature brilliance and power and grace. An essential, heartbreaking project." —Carmen Maria Machado, author of *Her Body and Other Parties* and *In the Dream House*

"Melissa Febos is part poet, part theorist, and all writer. In this lyrical, searching, profound, and personal collection, Febos examines childhood, femaleness, and love in its many forms with a sensuous ferocity that is all her own." —Ariel Levy, author of *The Rules Do Not Apply*

"Blazes through the stories we've been told with a dazzling fury and a brilliant beauty. Whatever we are or were, this is a map to a new becoming . . . A fuck-all guide to resilience and reclamation, a breathtaking reimagination of who we might be in spite of what we've been told. *Girlhood* will bring you back to life." —Lidia Yuknavitch, author of *The Book of Joan* and *Verge*

"An exquisite collection . . . Febos' insight is devastating, the examinations of her world—from the female body, queerness, consent, slut-shaming, and intimacy—are rigorous and compassionate. This is a book for mothers, daughters, and our deepest selves, a true light in the dark." —Stephanie Danler, author of *Sweetbitter* and *Stray*

"A gorgeously written, perfectly calibrated investigation into the traps, paths, and challenges of being female in this world. It's a stunner of a book." —Jami Attenberg, author of *All This Could Be Yours*

"American patriarchy teaches so many of us to hate our own bodies and stifle our own desires—to make ourselves smaller in every way. *Girlhood* is a smart, fierce, gloriously sensual critique of these lessons by a writer who has fought hard to unlearn them. Thank you, Melissa Febos, for charting this magnificent route of queer feminist resistance!" —Leni Zumas, author of *Red Clocks*

"Reading *Girlhood* felt like having a spell whispered into my ear. 'You carve yourself,' Melissa Febos writes, and the phrase becomes command, elegy, incantation. In these pages she conjures not only the past, but an allegory of experience at once universal and exquisitely personal. Intimate, urgent, and stunningly beautiful, this is a book that will be passed from hand to hand, from heart to heart." —Alex Marzano-Lesnevich, author *The Fact of a Body*

"At once intimate and didactic, lyric and wise, *Girlhood* is a must-read hybrid text for women looking to define themselves from the inside. This book is an exorcism of social messaging and external gazes, and Febos is a warm and erudite exorcist." —Melissa Broder, author of *The Pisces* and *Milk Fed*

"Lucid and timely . . . Febos's wit and sincerity push aside tropes of purity to make room for stories of real power and desire. The great surprise of the book is how masterfully she reinvents the path to womanhood, a philosopher's eye turned protectively toward the tenderest parts of the writer's former self." —Wendy S. Walters, author of *Multiply/Divide*

GIRLHOOD

Essays

MELISSA FEBOS

With illustrations by Forsyth Harmon

BLOOMSBURY PUBLISHING
NEW YORK · LONDON · OXFORD · NEW DELHI · SYDNEY

FOR MOM, TO WHOM I OWE EVERYTHING
AND FROM WHOM I HEARD ALL OF IT FIRST

BLOOMSBURY PUBLISHING
Bloomsbury Publishing Inc.
1385 Broadway, New York, NY 10018, USA

BLOOMSBURY, BLOOMSBURY PUBLISHING, and the Diana logo are
trademarks of Bloomsbury Publishing Plc

First published in the United States 2021
This edition published 2022

ISBN: HB: 978-1-63557-252-0; PB: 978-1-63557-931-4; eBook: 978-1-63557-253-7

LIBRARY OF CONGRESS CATALOGING-IN-PUBLICATION DATA IS AVAILABLE

4 6 8 10 9 7 5 3

Typeset by Westchester Publishing Services
Printed and bound in the U.S.A.

Destruction is thus always restoration—that is, the destruction of a set of categories that introduce artificial divisions into an otherwise unified ontology.

—Judith Butler, *Gender Trouble*

To say: no person, trying to take responsibility for her or his identity, should have to be so alone. There must be those among whom we can sit down and weep, and still be counted as warriors. (I make up this strange, angry packet for you, threaded with love.) I think you thought there was no such place for you, and perhaps there was none then, and perhaps there is none now; but we will have to make it, we who want an end to suffering, who want to change the laws of history, if we are not to *give ourselves away.*

—Adrienne Rich, "Sources"

CONTENTS

The story went like this: I was a happy child, if also a strange one. There were griefs, but I was safe and well-loved. The age of ten or eleven—the time when my childhood became more distinctly a *girl*hood—marked a violent turn from this. Everyone knows that adolescents rebel, girls in particular. Still, my own girlhood felt tinged by a darkness that the story of adolescent rebellion did not suffice to explain. In the years since, I have worried the question: What was wrong with me? I did not deserve to have been so tormented.

Despite how unspeakable it felt at the time, I no longer think that the pains or darkness of my own girlhood were exceptional. It is a darker time for many than we are often willing to acknowledge. During it, we learn to adopt a story about ourselves—what our value is, what beauty is, what is harmful and what is normal—and to privilege the feelings, comfort, perceptions, and power of others over our own. This training of our minds can lead to the exile of many parts of the self, to hatred for and the abuse of our own bodies, the policing of other girls, and a lifetime of allegiance to values that do not prioritize our safety, happiness, freedom, or pleasure. Though mine was among the last girlhoods untouched by the internet, I have found many of the same challenges among those who've grown up since.

For years, I considered it impossible to undo much of this indoctrination. Knowing about it was not enough. But I have found its undoing more possible than I suspected. The same way that I have taught my mind and my body to collaborate in a habitual set of practices that eventually coalesce into a skill that can be strengthened, such as throwing a softball, singing, jogging long distances, or writing—so I have found it possible to train my mind to act in accordance with *my* beliefs (and sometimes to discover what those are). Like any process of conditioning, it is tedious, minute, and demands rigorous attention. It cannot be done alone.

It is in part by writing this book that I have corrected the story of my own girlhood and found ways to recover myself. I have found company in the stories of other women, and the revelation of all our ordinariness has itself been curative. Writing has always been a way to reconcile my lived experience with the narratives available to describe it (or lack thereof). My hope is that these essays do some of that work for you, too.

—Melissa Febos

March 2020

New York, New York

Your
father
once gave
you a
picture
book
of knots

PROLOGUE
SCARIFICATION

1. First, the knees. They meet the gravel, the street, the blunt hips of curbs. Pain is the bright light flashing, forgotten for Vega's colors, then Halley's Comet—a burning streak behind the clouds. Your father holds you up to the sky, tells you, *Look.* Tells you, *Remember this.* You, small animal in the pink dress from your abuela, dirty sneakers, bloody knees, looking up.

2. The oven is eye level and your forearms striped with burns. A tally of each time you reach over your depth. Are you just a child, or already Einstein's definition of insanity? You like to be marked. Your mother, though, wails when she drops a blueberry pie from that height, sinks into the gory glory of its mess just before your father leaves port again. Oh, to stripe the floor with your own scalding compote. You stay closed, you hot box, you little teapot. You fill, but never empty. You stay striped.

3. They call it a faggot test. Do you know what a faggot is, or only that you are part boy? Rub the pencil's pink end

across the back of your hand until it erases you. The circle of boys claps when you draw blood. After school, your mother's stricken face scares you, but later, you are glad she saw the peeled pink of it—saw that it was in you.

4. Your best friend flowers your limbs with bruises—Indian sunburn, snake bite, monkey bite, her pale knuckles vised into your thigh. Her fingernails carve you, one time permanently. Only your body flinches. You know the need to engrave things. After baseball practice, still in cleats, when she presses her mouth against your neck under the mildewed blanket in your basement, you are sorry her hot mouth leaves no mark.

5. Your mother watches you watch a boy on your baseball team. She never meets your first love, a Cape Verdean boy to whom you barely speak. *Verdean, verdant*, you whisper, craving sounds that fill your mouth. *What are you?* he asks, as so many have. You whisper *cerulean, figlia, Melitta, querida*. You are nothing, just a shard beating the shore. Just a small animal you fling into the sea. Behind the mall, break dancers spin on sheets of cardboard, and from that circle of boys, he throws a rock that finds your face. Blood on your mouth, you call your father from a pay phone. Baseball at dusk? *You know better*, he says, though he is proud. He has coached your teams since Little League. He wraps ice packs in dish towels, makes

you hold them against the new scar. Your eyes blacken anyway.

6. In the locker room, you perfect the art of changing your clothes under your clothes. Your body is a secret you keep, a white rabbit, and you the magician who disappears it. Remember: this is a hard hustle to break. It is difficult to keep some secrets and not others. Hustle now, across that field, forgetting your body as only this allows, and reach for the ball that scorches your hand with pain. See what happens when you forget yourself? It is better to choose your pain than to let it choose you.

7. In the tiny bathroom of your father's house, you tuck your fingers into your mouth until sweat beads your body and your throat bitters. All day, you rub your tongue against the scraped inside, the bitten knuckle. You are sore for days, but it doesn't keep. You choose it, and then it chooses you.

8. At sixteen, you shave your head, disappointed that no curb or wall or rock has altered its perfect sphere. Your father's stricken face pleases you. When you pierce your nose, he tells you no one will ever see your face again for the glare. You don't tell him that's the point. When he looks at you, he sees only the message you carry, written in a language he never taught you, not Spanish, but the other language of his childhood, the one that leaves marks. You quit baseball and move out of his house.

9. Instead of ten holes, your body now has twenty-three. You stop returning your father's phone calls. You don't listen to his messages. At night, you touch each opening, drawing the constellation of your body: Lyra, Libra, Big Dipper, flickering Vega, binary Mizar, you bucket of light, you horse and rider. You lick your fingers and tuck them inside, tug on these mouths and others, the knots of skin between you, and you, and you.

10. The first time, you look away as your lover slides the needle into the crook of your arm. Your body beads with sweat and your throat bitters. You choose it—this pale boy, this new hole, this fill, this empty, this orphaning— and then it chooses you.

11. Your father once gave you a picture book of knots, a smooth length of rope looped around its spine. *Half Hitch, Figure Eight, Clove Hitch, Bowline, Anchor Bend, Slip Knot.* The only one you remember the first time you tie two wrists together is a square knot, but it's the only one you need. The first time a man pays to tie your wrists, he doesn't know right over left, left over right. Only a Better Bow, rabbit in the hole, but not disappeared. Every time, you slip away—pinched nerves, pinked thighs, wax stars sealing your dark parts. They tuck their fingers into your mouth and tug until your body beads with sweat

and your throat bitters. You choose them, and then they choose you.

12. Like you, he is part feral, part vessel. Nights, he tucks into the curve of you, sings a rippled sigh across your pillow. In sleep you burn, a glowing ember, soaking the sheets. You wake sticky-chested, heart a drum, and listen to him cry. You clench his twitching paws. Like you, he fears his own kind and leads with his teeth. You fling yourself into his fights—tooth to knuckle, street to knee, and you never make a sound, forget yourself as only this allows. After, you touch each opening with trembling hands, drawing the constellation of this animal: Sirius, dog star, Polaris, and you Orioned with bloody hands. You pick the gravel out of your knees, wince every time you close your hand, but he makes you a hunter.

13. The year your father leaves port for the last time, you draw the needle out. Your body beads with sweat and your throat bitters. In sleep, you burn, and wake shaking wet. Remember this supernova, you black hole, you cosmic shard, your dark matter spilling out. When it lifts, you are peeled pink, pain the bright light flashing, but in it you see everything.

14. You don't choose her but she finds you, smooth shard, and tucks you away. In love, your hair and fingernails grow

bone-bright, wax-white, needle-thin, then tear off and fall away. You run. Marked thing, you run until your knees throb, toenails loosen, skull's bowl tipping open. You fling yourself against her. You wear yourself away. Hot ember in her hands, you glow. At night, she touches every opening, drawing the constellation of your burning body, and when you leave her, it finally cools.

15. This time, you choose the needle and the hand that holds it. You carve the things you want to remember into your shoulder, your hip, the crook of your arm. You carve yourself into paper. These are not secrets, but they keep. You bare these new marks and your father says nothing, but he looks at you. You look, too, and finally, you both see it. Cepheus and Andromeda, Mizar and Alcor, Zeus and Athena, you binary creatures, you star and sextant, navigator and horizon. You draw the constellation of your history, connecting the dots of your heavenly body. This is your celestial heart. You choose it, and it chooses you.

I dangled my feet into that
colder depth and shivered.

"What do you like?" the men would ask. "Spitting," I'd say. To even utter the word felt like the worst kind of cuss, and I trained myself not to flinch or look away or offer a compensatory smile after I said it. In the dungeon's dim rooms, I unlearned my instinct for apology. I learned to hold a gaze. I learned the pleasure of cruelty.

It was not true cruelty, of course. My clients paid $75 an hour to enact their disempowerment. The sex industry is a service industry, and I served humiliation to order. But the pageant of it was the key. To spit in an unwilling face was inconceivable to me and still is. But at a man who had paid for it?

They knelt at my feet. They crawled naked across gleaming wood floors. They begged to touch me, begged for forgiveness. I refused. I leaned over their plaintive faces and gathered the wet in my mouth. I spat. Their hard flinch, eyes clenched. The shock of it radiated through my body, then settled, then swelled into something else.

"Do you hate men?" people sometimes asked.

"Not at all," I answered.

"You must work out a lot of anger that way," they suggested.

"I never felt angry in my sessions," I told them. I often explained that the dominatrix's most useful tool was a well-developed empathic sense. What I did not acknowledge to any curious stranger, or to myself, was that empathy and anger are not mutually exclusive.

We are all unreliable narrators of our own motives. And feeling something neither proves nor disproves its existence. Conscious feelings are no accurate map to the psychic imprint of our experiences; they are the messy catalog of emotions once and twice and thrice removed, often the symptoms of what we won't let ourselves feel. They are not *Jane Eyre*'s locked-away Bertha Mason, but her cries that leak through the floorboards, the fire she sets while we sleep and the wet nightgown of its quenching.

I didn't derive any sexual pleasure from spitting, I assured people. Only psychological. Now, this dichotomy seems flimsy at best. How is the pleasure of giving one's spit to another's hungry mouth not sexual? I needed to distinguish that desire from what I might feel with a lover. I wanted to divorce the pleasure of violence from that of sex. But that didn't make it so.

It was the thrill of transgression, I said. Of occupying a male space of power. It was the exhilaration of doing the thing

I would never do, was forbidden to do by my culture and by my conscience. I believed my own explanations, though now it is easy to poke holes in them.

I did not want to be angry. What did I have to be angry about? My clients sought catharsis through the reenactment of childhood traumas. They were hostages to their pasts, to the people who had disempowered them. I was no such hostage—I did not even want to consider it. I wanted only to be brave and curious and in control. I did not want my pleasure to be any kind of redemption. One can only redeem a thing that has already been lost or taken. I did not want to admit that someone had taken something from me.

His name was Alex, and he lived at the end of a long unpaved driveway off the same wooded road that my family did. It took ten minutes to walk between our homes, both of which sat on the bank of Deep Pond. Like many of the ponds on Cape Cod, ours formed some fifteen thousand years ago when a block of ice broke from a melting glacier and drove deep into the solidifying land of my future backyard. When the ice block melted, the deep depression filled with water and became what is called a kettle-hole lake.

Despite its small circumference, our pond plummeted fifty feet at its deepest point. My brother and I and all the children raised on the pond spent our summers getting wet, chasing one another through invented games, our happy screams garbled with water. I often swam out to the deepest point—not the center of the pond, but to its left—and trod water over this heart cavity. In summer, the sun warmed the surface to bath temperatures, but a few feet deeper it went cold. Face warm, arms flapping, I dangled my feet into that colder depth and shivered. Fifty feet was taller than any building in our town, was more than ten of me laid head to foot. It was a mystery big enough to hold a whole city. I could swim in it my whole life and never know what lay at its bottom.

An entry in my diary from age ten announces: "Today Alex came over and swam with us. I think he likes me."

Alex was a grade ahead of me and a foot taller. He had a wide mouth, tapered brown eyes, and a laugh that brayed clouds in the chill of fall mornings at our bus stop. He wore the same shirt for four out of five school days, and I thought he was beautiful. I had known Alex for years, but that recorded swim is the first clear memory I have of him. A few months later, he spat on me for the first time.

When I turned eleven, I enrolled in the public middle school with all the other fifth- and sixth-graders in our town. The new bus stop was farther down the wooded road, where it ended at the perpendicular intersection of another. On that corner was a large house, owned by Robert Ballard, the oceanographer who discovered the wreck of the *Titanic* in 1985. Early in his career, Ballard had worked with the nearby Woods Hole Oceanographic Institution, and it was during his deepsea dives off the coast of Massachusetts that his obsession with shipwrecks was born. Sometimes I studied that house—its many gleaming windows and ivy-choked tennis court—and thought about the difference between Ballard and my father, who was a captain in the merchant marines. One man carried his cargo across oceans; the other ventured deep inside them to discover his. I was drawn to the romance of each: to slice across the glittering surface, and also to plunge into the cold depths. A stone wall wrapped around Ballard's yard. Here, we waited for the school bus.

I read books as I walked to the bus stop. Reading ate time. Whole hours disappeared in stretches. It shortened the length of my father's voyages, moved me closer to his returns with every page. I was a magician with a single power: to disappear the world. I emerged from whole afternoons of reading, my life a foggy half-dream through which I drifted as my self bled back into me like steeping tea.

The start of fifth grade marked more change than the location of my bus stop. My parents had separated that summer.

My body, that once reliable vessel, began to transform. But what emerged from it was no happy magic, no abracadabra. It went kaboom. The new body was harder to disappear.

"I wish people didn't change sometimes," I wrote in my diary. By people, I meant my parents. I meant me. I meant the boy who swam across that lake toward my new body with its power to compel but not control.

Before puberty, I moved through the world and toward other people without hesitance or self-consciousness. I read hungrily and kept lists of all the words I wanted to look up in a notebook with a red velvet cover. I still have the notebook. "Ersatz," it reads. "Entropy. Mnemonic. Morass. Corpulent. Hoary." I was smart and strong and my power lay in these things alone. My parents loved me well and mirrored these strengths back to me.

Perhaps more so than other girls', my early world was a safe one. My mother banned cable TV and sugar cereals, and made feminist corrections to my children's books with a Sharpie. When he was home from sea, my father taught me how to throw a baseball and a punch, how to find the North Star, and start a fire. I was protected from the darker leagues of what it meant to be female. I think now of the *Titanic*—not the familiar tragedy of its wreck, the scream of ice against her starboard flank, the thunder of seawater gushing through her cracked hull. I think of the short miracle of her passage. The 375 miles she floated, immaculate, across the Atlantic. My early passage was a miracle, too. Like the *Titanic*'s, it did not last.

My mother noticed first. "Your body is a temple," she told me. But the bra she bought me felt more straitjacket than vestment. I wore baggy T-shirts and hunched my shoulders. I tried to bury my body. It was too big in all the wrong ways. My hips went purple from crashing them into table corners; I no longer knew my own shape. My mother brought home a book called *The What's Happening to My Body? Book for Girls*. It explained hormonal shifts, the science of breasts and pubic hair. It was not *The What's Happening to the World as I Knew It? Book for Girls* and did not explain why being the only girl on the baseball team no longer felt like a triumph. It did not explain why grown men in passing cars, to whom I had always been happily invisible, now leered at me. It did not explain why or even acknowledge that what was happening to my body changed my value in the world.

I did not ask about these other changes. Maybe some children do. But what if I asked and my parents did not have answers? It already seemed a risk to reveal myself. If the changes I felt were not indexed in the book they gave me, perhaps they were mine alone.

Children know so little of the world. Every new thing might be our own creation. If a logic is not given, we invent one. How would my mother have explained it to me, at ten? I can't imagine.

One autumn afternoon, Alex invited me and my little brother to his house to play soccer. I was not a soccer player, but I dragged my little brother down the road and up that dirt driveway to where Alex and his cousin kicked the ball back and forth across the patchy grass. The sky hung low over his dusty yard and silvery clouds ripened overhead. At eleven, I could still win a race against the boys on my baseball team. Even holding my T-shirt tented in front of my chest, I could win. They still called me Mrs. Babe Ruth. But Alex was a year older than me and twice as big. He did not let me win.

He pummeled the net with goals. He kicked the ball so hard that I jumped out of its path, then burned with shame and chased it into the woods.

"Eat that!" he sneered and spat into the cloud of dust kicked up by our feet. He sauntered back to his side of our makeshift field and swiped his forehead with the hem of his T-shirt, baring his flat stomach, ridged with muscle.

An hour into our game, the sky broke, dumping water onto our dusty field. Alex didn't stop, so neither did I. I ran, wet hair plastered to my face and neck. My oversize T-shirt clung to my chest, translucent and sopping. Even that didn't stop me. I ran, thighs burning, lungs heaving, mud splattered up the legs of my jeans. Alex was a machine, dribbling the ball through inches-deep puddles of mud, driving it into our goal. He barely looked at me, but every kick felt personal, aimed at my body. I did not understand what we were fighting for, only that I could not surrender.

I drilled into that day with everything I had, and it was not enough. Not even close. It was the last day that I believed my body's power lay in its strength.

Twenty-five years later, I read that day's entry in my diary. "Today," I wrote, "I played soccer at Alex's house for FOUR HOURS! It was SO FUN!"

It was not fun. It was a humiliation. It was a mystery. It was a punishment, though I did not know for what. The instinct in me to hide it was so strong that I lied in my diary. I wanted no record of that wreck.

The *Titanic* was named after the Greek Titans, an order of divine beings that preceded the Olympic deities. I loved Greek mythology as a girl, and among my favorite gods was

Mnemosyne, a Titaness and the mother of the Muses. According to fourth-century B.C. Greek texts, the dead were given a choice to drink either from the river Lethe, which would erase their memories of the life before reincarnation, or from the river Mnemosyne, and carry those memories with them into the next life. In his *Aeneid*, Virgil wrote that the dead could not achieve reincarnation without forgetting. At the age of twelve, I had made my choice.

The other regulars on the stone wall of our bus stop were two girls, Sarah and Chloe. They were also a grade ahead of me. Sarah was blond and nervous. Chloe and Alex were cousins.

Alex had ignored all three of us at our previous bus stop, but not anymore. Sometimes he whispered to one girl about the other two, mean words that we laughed at with the faint hysteria of relief that it was not our turn. He teased Chloe about boys in their class or how small she was. Once, he picked her up and pretended to throw her over the stone wall.

"Stop it, Alex!" she shouted. She blushed furiously and rolled her eyes while Sarah and I envied her. Sarah blanched when bullied, and we could immediately see the crumple behind her face that preceded tears. Alex always stopped before she cried. Eventually, he didn't bother with her anymore. With me he was relentless.

My insults were not as effective, but I always fought back. He challenged me to contests, with Sarah as the enthusiastic judge. Races that I could never win. Staring contests. Arm wrestling matches in which we knelt in the damp grass and he slammed the back of my hand onto the stone wall's surface. He pretended it was a game or a joke, and though they all laughed, we knew it wasn't. There was none of the coddling he gave to Chloe or the caution with which he approached Sarah. Still, I would not accept victimhood. Though I woke filled with sickening dread every morning and went to sleep with it every night, to tell my mother or ask her to drive me to school was unthinkable; the idea was abhorrent to me.

I was the daughter of a sea captain. I would not be rescued. Idiom, maritime tradition, and even law have insisted that the captain goes down with the ship. The rule implies a sense of responsibility both to the rescue of a captain's passengers and to his pride. Captain Edward Smith of the *Titanic* was seen on the ship's bridge moments before it was engulfed in water. My own stubbornness reflected this same ethos—to protect my tenderest wards, or go down trying, alone.

One day he began chasing me. I don't know what he planned to do if he caught me, and I don't think he knew either. To my relief, the bus arrived before we found out. He chased me up the bus steps but stopped short behind me and strolled past as I slid into a seat. I didn't realize that he'd spat on me until I felt the wet between my hair and the vinyl bus seat. I reached behind my head and pulled my fingers away, wiping them on the leg of my jeans as I stared out the bus window. I felt a new sensation in my chest, behind my breastbone. It pulled, a hand gathering cloth.

The second time, I spat back. Over a period of weeks, he spat in my hair, my face, my books, my backpack. I rarely got him back, but I always tried. Once, I dodged him well enough to board the bus behind him, unscathed. At the last minute, as I stepped onto the bus, he bounded back down the aisle and hocked a great wad of mucus onto my cheek.

I knew that if I gave in to tears or stopped fighting back, he would stop. I could not. My defiance matched my suffering.

One afternoon I did not see him on the bus after school and realized, with tentative relief, that I would not have to fight my way home. I hurried off the bus to get a head start on Sarah and Chloe, uninterested in the conversation that we three might share in his absence. I retrieved my book from my backpack as I passed the end of Alex's street.

I felt him behind me before I heard him. I flinched so hard and my despair came so fast and strong that I did not have time to steel myself before the tears fell. I pushed out a single, gasped "Fuck you," but could not form words after that. He followed silently, watching me in profile. I raised my book between our faces to block his view. He pushed it down.

"I'm sorry," he said. I cried harder, my breath stuttering, and raised my book again. He pushed it down again. "I didn't know it bothered you," he said. "I wouldn't do it if I didn't think you could take it," he said. "It's not because I don't like you," he said. "I do."

I believed him. Superstition makes Greek fishermen spit three times in their nets before setting sail, to ward off evil. King Minos forced the seer Polyidus to teach his foolish son magic, and when granted freedom, the philosopher asked the fool to spit into his mouth, to make him forget. Perhaps there is no spit given without desire, without a fear of powers enormous enough to destroy you. But Alex's mouth was my awakening. In some inchoate way, I understood that desire led to fear that could lead to hate—all without ever obliterating that original want. It was a power struggle that would take me twenty more years to truly understand.

After that day, Alex let me be. I read my books at the bus stop. But I understood something new. That he had wanted something from me and hated me for it. That there was nothing I could have given or withheld or done to change that. In the year that followed, I came to better understand the lessons about my female body, the ones that tell us punishment is a reward, that disempowerment is power. I quit baseball. When one of the boys I used to play with wanted to put his hands under my clothes, I did not stop him. Perhaps to let them win was the better way, after all.

The other girls at school pranced in bathing suits in carpeted basements in front of huge televisions. They stuffed their mothers' bras and mimicked the poses of models in lingerie magazines. They talked endlessly about the boys who'd begun calling my house in the evening. At twelve, I already had a body like those women in the magazines, but it was no prize and they offered me no congratulations. It was a race that I had won without trying, and to win it was the greatest loss of all.

Eventually I understood the strength that was no strength, that was a punishment no matter what I did or did not do. So I let my friend's older brother close the closet door. I let the persistent older boy dig under my clothes and between my legs. My once-strong body became a passive thing, tossed and splintered, its corners rounded from use. Unrecognizable.

There was a pleasure in compelling them. The way they could not stay away. But as soon as they touched me, it was gone. I had no control over what happened next, the names they called me in school, the crude gestures, the prank phone calls—not even when my mother answered the phone. She wanted to help me, but I had no words for what was happening. My chambers were breached. They filled with that weight. I was sunk.

How could she have prepared me for this? You cannot win against an ocean. There is no good strategy in a rigged game. There are only new ways to lose.

There was a difference between my body in the world and my body at home. At eleven, I soaked in the bath, a damp book in one hand, the other lazily exploring the tender handfuls of my breasts and new bloom of my hips, the soft pocket of my sex. The first time I slid on my back to the bottom of the tub, propped my heels on the wall aside the faucet and let that hot water pummel me, I understood that to crack my own hull was a glory, a power summoned instead of submerged. Alone, I was both ship and sea, and I felt no shame, only the cascade of pleasure, my body shuddering against the smooth porcelain.

I stole *My Secret Garden* from my mother's bedroom bookshelf and kept it tucked under my mattress. Nancy Friday's 1973 volume of real women's fantasies is organized by headings that include "The Lesbians," "Anonymity," "Rape," and "The Zoo." I came to all of them, even the one story about a woman who fucks a dog. I felt no embarrassment or shock at the stories nor at my own pleasure. Only orgasm after orgasm. I discovered that after the first one I could come again and again and again with only seconds in between—a capacity no lover discovered for another twenty years. I came on my back, my belly, straddling my pillows. I came with the handle of a wooden hairbrush inside me, a carrot, a cucumber, the plastic leg of a doll. I tasted my new wetness, the consistency of spit, but salted and sweet. I came on my knees on my bedroom floor with a hand mirror between my legs.

Alone in my bedroom, my body was miles deeper than I had ever fathomed. Under my hands, it quaked from floor to tidal swell. The world was more enormous than I had known, its power crushing. I was also enormous, I found, a seething world of which men knew so little.

After the prank phone calls, after the pull in my chest grew so familiar I couldn't tell if it was in me or *was* me, after my father read my diary and the long cold catalog of every boy that touched me but never how little I felt under their hands, after the screaming fights about where I had really spent my

Saturday afternoon, after they found the liquor bottles in my sock drawer, after they changed the phone number and sent me to private school for a year, but shortly before I started kissing girls, I went back to public school in eighth grade and returned to Ballard's stone wall.

This time, when Alex kept walking beside me past his own street and led me into the woods across from my family's mailbox, I knew what he wanted. We lay in the damp leaves, twigs cracking under us, amid the smell of pine needles and dirt. I stared up at the spires of treetops, the green glowed stars of leaves, and listened to the coo of mourning doves.

There, Alex covered my mouth with his. Though we had traded spit before, ours had never mingled like this. For the first time, I tasted that mixture of desire and violence. It had always been both. He pushed my T-shirt up over my belly and chest, where it bunched in my armpits. I let him. It was a thing I had done many times before, or let be done to me. This time it filled me with a terrible sadness. In those woods where I had played all my life, so close to my own home, the bright flicker of light on the pond nearly visible through the trees, it felt as though I was killing something, or letting him kill it. Still, I did not stop him. Eventually, he stopped on his own. I sat up and pulled down my shirt. We parted without speaking.

I knew we would never speak of it, might never speak again. I didn't care. I didn't want anything from him, except what he'd already taken.

Bob Ballard always dreamed of finding the *Titanic*. As a boy, he had idolized Captain Nemo. I used to imagine the glory of that moment when he discovered it. How magnificent it must have looked, the hulking remains seventy years buried on the ocean floor, one thousand miles out to sea from where I grew up. The glory of that moment was dampened, Ballard later claimed, by the sobering reality that it was a gravesite he'd found. Fifteen hundred people died in the wreck, and when his crew found it, they could see where the bodies had fallen.

What if they hadn't known about those bodies? What if Ballard had not even been searching for the *Titanic* when he found it? A mystery solved is always a death: that of possibility, denial, the dream of our own invincibility.

I believed all the reasons that I gave for ending up in the dungeon. That the pleasure I took from spitting in men's faces was no kind of redemption. I did not think of Alex until years later, when I was writing a book about having been a dominatrix. I was a grown woman, alone at my desk. When I remembered—the flinch I would not give him, the terrible clutching dread—I became that girl with her feet dangled into the cold of Deep Pond, then suddenly touching down. I saw it all, my own ghosted wreck glowing at the bottom.

In the dungeon, my identity was distilled once again to its objective meaning. Those men, like all the men before them, prescribed my body's uses. This time, my job was to deny instead of acquiesce, to say no instead of yes. Maybe it was the best way to learn how to form those sounds in my own mouth.

"I want you," they said over and over.

"You cannot have me," I replied every time.

"Please," they insisted.

"No," I said. Like Charybdis chained to the ocean floor, I spat the sea into their eyes and roared. "No. No. No. No. No." Inside those two letters stretched a fifty-foot microcosm, a world over which I had treaded water for decades. I had not known how tired I was until I stopped. Then, I grew strong. What more perfect a redemption could I have designed? I did not have to understand it to enjoy it. When I did understand, I felt as I imagine Ballard must have when he glimpsed his *Titanic* for the first time.

I saw Alex once. Years later, when I was a domme, or shortly thereafter. One sunny summer afternoon on the porch of his brother's house. He looked the same. He would not look at me, though I ached to show him this new me, this mistress of *no*. In that wish was the knowledge of my still-soft parts, how they shook in his presence, how innocent they remained.

They say that to love someone else, you have to love yourself first. It is not true. Being loved, the relentless care of my family, my lovers, my friends, has sewn me back together. Sometimes the warmth of a mouth that loves me is enough to break me open, to unravel all that careful control. I am shocked and so relieved to find that I am still soft inside. That I can give my body to a lover and still keep it for myself. It is that lost girl they love, too, whether I can or not.

When I think back to that boy, his big hands and wet mouth, sometimes I want to go back, to tell him *no*, to preserve the piece of me that was driven deep underground. More than anything, I want to apologize to that girl. How could she have known? She survived the best way she knew how. The true telling of our stories often requires the annihilation of other stories, the ones we build and carry through our lives because it is easier to preserve some mysteries. We don't need the truth to survive, and sometimes our survival depends on its denial.

That wreck appeared to me both magnificent and tragic. How had I hidden it for so long? It did feel like a gravesite. Not of anything that Alex had killed in me, but of something I had killed in my burying. Whatever river you drink from, forgetting does not erase your past. It only hides what wrecks you carry into the next life.

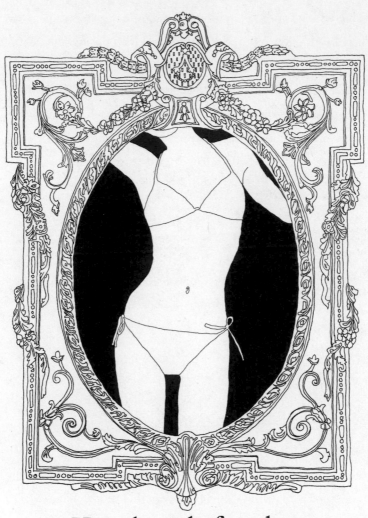

How long before her
reflection replaces herself?

THE MIRROR TEST

What is truth? Where a woman is concerned,
it's the story that's easiest to believe.
—Edith Wharton, *The House of Mirth*

1

When I teach Jamaica Kincaid's short story "Girl," which I do a few times each year, I often play for the class a video of the author reading her work at the 2015 Chicago Humanities Festival. The story consists of a single long paragraph composed of imperative statements made by an implied mother character. Between instructions for domestic tasks like how to properly launder clothes and set a table are those for not behaving or appearing like "the slut you are so bent on becoming"—a phrase that recurs throughout the story. In the recording, each time Kincaid repeats this line—the word *slut* a glittering shard in the smooth putty of her voice—the audience laughs. There is nothing about the story or the refrain, nor in the author's countenance, that implies humor.

"This is how you set a table for tea," the mother explains. "This is how you sweep a whole house." Bread, she tells the girl, should always be squeezed to ascertain its freshness, *"but what if the baker won't let me feel the bread?*; you mean to say that after all you are really going to be the kind of woman who the baker won't let near the bread?"

In the eighteenth century, "slut's pennies" were hard nuggets in a loaf of bread that resulted from incomplete kneading. I imagine them salty and dense, soft enough to sink your tooth into, but tough enough to stick. What could a handful of slut's pennies buy you? Nothing—a hard word, a slap in the face, a fast hand for your slow ones.

Before it carried any sexual connotation, the word *slut* was a term for a slovenly woman, a poor housekeeper. A slut was the maid who left dust on the floor—"slut's wool"—or who left a corner of the room overlooked in her cleaning—a "slut's corner"—or who let dirt collect in a sewer or hole in a ground—"a slut's hole." An untidy man might occasionally be referred to as "sluttish," but for his sloppy jacket, not his unswept floor, because a slut was a doer of menial house-work, a drudge, a maid, a servant—a woman.

A slut was a careless girl, hands sunk haphazardly into the dough, broom stilled against her shoulder—eyes cast out the window, mouth humming a song, always thinking of some-thing else.

Oh, was I ever a messy child. A real slut in the making. My clothes entangled on the floor; my books splayed open and dog-eared, their bindings split. Dirty dishes on the bookshelf, sticky spoons glued to the rug. I would never have bathed if not commanded.

At a certain point, when I got in trouble and wanted to be seen as good again, I would clean my room. But only when I wanted to be good, not because I wanted to be clean. I already understood that goodness was something you earned, that existed only in the esteem of others. Alone in my room, I was always good. Or, I was never good. It was not a thing to care about alone in my room, unless I was thinking about the people outside and the ways I might need them to see me.

The story goes like this: In March 1838, Darwin visited the Zoological Society of London's gardens. The zoo had just acquired Jenny, a female orangutan. The scientist watched a zookeeper tease the ape with an apple. Jenny flung herself on the ground in frustration, "precisely like a naughty child." Later, he watched her study a mirror in her cage. The visit led him to wonder about the animal's emotional landscape. Did she have a sense of fairness to offend? Did she feel wronged, and what sense of selfhood would such a reaction imply? What did Jenny recognize in her own reflection?

More than a century later, Darwin's musings led to the mirror test, developed in 1970 by the psychologist Gordon Gallup Jr. It is sometimes called the mirror self-recognition test (MSR), and is used to assess an animal's ability to visually recognize itself. In it, an animal is marked with a sticker or paint in an area it cannot normally see. Then it is shown a mirror. If the animal subsequently investigates the mark on its own body, it is seen to perform this self-recognition. Great apes, Eurasian magpies, bottlenose dolphins, orcas, ants, and one Asian elephant are the most frequently cited animals to have passed the test.

Just think of all the things a woman could do rather than clean. Which is to say, think of all the pastimes that might make her a slut: reading; talking; listening; thinking; masturbating; eating; observing the sky, the ground, other people, or herself; picking a scab; smoking; painting; building something; daydreaming; sleeping; hatching a plan; conspiring; laughing; communing with animals; communing with God; imagining herself a god; imagining a future in which her time is her own.

In Samuel Johnson's 1755 dictionary (the precursor to the *Oxford English*) a slut is simply a dirty woman, without any sexual connotation. In the nineteenth century, a slut also becomes a female dog, and a rag dipped in lard to light in place of a candle. Though in the twentieth century its meaning solidifies as an immoral woman, a woman with the morals of a man, it isn't until the 1960s that a slut finally becomes a sexually promiscuous woman, "a woman who enjoys sex in a degree considered shamefully excessive."

It is a brilliant linguistic trajectory. Make the bad housekeeper a woman of poor morals. Make her maid service to men a moral duty, and every other act becomes a potentially immoral one. Make her a bitch, a dog, a pig, any kind of subservient or inferior beast. Create one word for them all. Make sex a moral duty, too, but pleasure in it a crime. This way you can punish her for anything. You can make her humanity monstrous. Now you can do anything you want to her.

One of the first orgasms I remember having was to the 1983 movie *Valley Girl*, starring Nicolas Cage. I was not interested in the chaste romance between Cage's punk Randy and Deborah Foreman's Valley girl Julie. There was a scene, however, in which Randy goes to the punk club and runs into his ex,

Samantha, a smoldering brunette. Their urgent exchange in the shadows of that club was so compelling that I ignored the fact of my grandmother dozing on the sofa behind me as I masturbated to climax, then again, and again, and again. I had no concept that my behavior might approach "a degree considered shamefully excessive."

Female pleasure or any indication of it was nowhere found in our school's sex ed curriculum. Wet dreams and male masturbation, of course. Boys, I knew, could masturbate excessively, though this cliché was treated with a kind of jocular resignation. "No one ever tried to hide a man's penis from him," writes Cara Kulwicki in her essay, "Real Sex Education." In order to talk about reproduction, sex ed curriculums can't avoid describing men's most common route to orgasm. Conversely, "women enter adulthood all too often without knowing what a clitoris is, where it is, and/or what to do with it," writes Kulwicki. Girls' sex ed was all periods and unwanted pregnancy. We learned how to put a condom on a banana, where our cervix and fallopian tubes were located on a simple anatomical diagram, but not how or even if women masturbated.

Tanaïs, a thirty-six-year-old artist I interviewed, articulates it easily: "Kids are sexual, you have to help them navigate that and not be like, ashamed of it, but also not be sexual, because it's not appropriate." But how difficult this is, in a culture that offers so many encouragements to be sexual and to feel ashamed of it. Good guidance most likely comes from someone who received it themselves and can easily be drowned out amid the cacophony of so many contradictory sources.

Despite the inherent sexism of our public school sex education, I suppose I am glad we were not preemptively shamed in class for our pleasure, that it was simply absent, left up to us to determine how it might be found in our bodies or situated in our lives and minds.

I was lucky to have no family or religious dogma that condemned sexual pleasure, and so my relationship to it had an untamed beginning. I was as enthusiastic and messy in exploring my body as I was in exploring the woods around our home, the murky bottom of the pond. No one was watching, and I was free of the consciousness of self that a gaze brings. An orgasm was a private thing, a firework in the dark of one's body.

The psychologist Henri Wallon observed that both humans and chimpanzees seem to recognize their own reflections around six months of age. In 1931 he published a paper in which he argued that mirrors aid in the development of a child's self-conception.

Five years later, Jacques Lacan presented his development of this idea at the Fourteenth Annual Psychoanalytical

Congress at Marienbad. He called it *le stade du miroir*, the mirror stage. Before it reaches the mirror stage, the infant is simply a conduit for its own experience. (The Lacanian baby is always male, adding yet another layer of distance for the female reader considering her self-conception, though I will close it here.) Self-conception is piecemeal—here is a foot, here a hand—but perhaps closer to what Lacan would later call the Real. There is no *I*. Experience is not mediated by significa-tion or perception. Then the baby sees herself in the mirror. The image of her own body disturbs and then delights her as she identifies with it. The self becomes unified and objectified simultaneously, and the uneasy grasping for a fixed subject begins. The baby cannot tell the difference between the mirror self and the actual self. It is the first story she tells herself about herself: that is me. It is the beginning of self-alienation.

In fourth grade, Vicki and I were friends, which meant that we attended sleepovers at each other's houses, played invented games during recess with the same group of girl classmates, and our mothers had each other's numbers. Vicki and I had the same birthday, though by the summer before fifth grade, I understood that our differences far outweighed our similari-ties. Vicki lived in a characterless mansion on the west side of our town, in a housing development of identical mansions.

I lived in a gray-shingled house in the woods with a tiny black-and-white television, and cabinets full of foods no one at school had ever heard of. Vicki had more Barbies than friends, and she was very popular. Most notably, Vicki had a pale white Popsicle body and freckled cheeks, while I was the first girl in our grade with breasts.

Vicki had an early pool party for her birthday—our birthday—but she didn't ask me to share it, and it didn't occur to me that she might have for many years. Now I can see how shrewd that choice, how better for both of us. How awkward it would have been for her to preside over both of our birthdays. In her spacious backyard, she commanded us as she did on the school playground, except on that day she did so in a pink bikini.

The other girls also scampered around her yard in their bathing suits, legs straight as clothespins, bellies bright white, chests flat and unmoving as they ran. I kept my T-shirt on. Underneath it I wore a bright green one-piece with a decorative zipper on the front, bought on sale at the T.J. Maxx in town, not the Gap or Puritan, places where I thought only rich people like Vicki shopped. I would have worn a snowsuit if I could.

As we sat around the patio table eating pizza, a girl complimented Vicki on her suit. Vicki waved dismissively as she took a bite and then swiped a dribble of grease from her chin with a paper napkin. We all watched her chew and then regally swallow.

"This is for babies without *boobs*," she explained. "When I have boobs, I'm going to get one of those suits with a zipper *right here*." She pointed coyly at her pink top. "And I'm going to unzip it all the way down to here." She dragged her finger down until the whole cohort laughed, even me, with my heart in my gut.

The role of the mirror stage is ultimately "to establish a relationship between an organism and its reality—or, as they say, between the *Innenwelt* and the *Umwelt*."

The baby, Lacan tells us, can see herself before she can control herself. It is this temporal dialectic that makes the mirror stage "a drama whose internal pressure pushes precipitously from insufficiency to anticipation." This fragmented self is reconciled by the creation of an anticipatory body, an "'orthopedic' form of its totality." The creation of a story about the body—*I will have boobs, I will have a bathing suit, I will unzip it all the way to here*—to reconcile the distance between the image of the self and the experience of the self allows us to move through space, to have a conception of identity that feels solid, though it is not. It is the construction of a fiction that will eventually harden into something else.

After presents, Vicki ordered us all into the pool. I lingered at the table and tried to demur, but she insisted and so I waded into the shallow end with my T-shirt on, its wet hem sticking to my thighs as the whole party watched.

"No, Melissa," Vicki shouted, exasperated. "Take your T-shirt off! You can't play with a T-shirt on." Someone giggled. I stared down at the blue water, my feet rippling at the bottom. Then I squeezed my eyes shut and pulled off my shirt.

No one said anything. They didn't have to. If I had hoped that it might be seen as luck—me in possession of that thing they all wanted, most of all Vicki—then my hope sank before my shirt hit the concrete. They stared at my zippered swimsuit. No, they stared at my body, and in those scorching moments—the blue water turned flame—I knew that there are some people we love for having the things we don't, and some people we hate for the same reason.

Though I spent hours staring in the mirror at that age, I hadn't yet learned how to see my own changed body. That afternoon I glimpsed her, a glimmering double that others could also see, that was the only thing they could see of me. Vicki and I never played again, not because what girls did at recess or on the weekends was no longer playing—instead a kind of work to become an impossible thing and to discipline the bodies that failed worst at this—but because she had recognized that we were different, a fact I'd already known. It would be another year before Alex would spit in my face, before Vicki or anyone would call me a slut, or threaten me, or prank-call my home, but by the time it happened, I already knew who they meant.

Gallup's mirror test answered the question of an animal's ability to recognize itself in its reflection, but it did not answer Darwin's first question: Did she have a sense of fairness to offend? Did she feel wronged, and what sense of selfhood did such a reaction imply? A sense of fairness and a capacity for feeling wronged seemed to suggest humanity to Darwin. The scientist's ultimate question about Jenny was always the same: How human is she? The acceptance of poor treatment has often been interpreted as a validation of such treatment, at least by its enactors, who are not interested in questioning their own humanity.

Queen Victoria, who visited the ape in May 1842, described Jenny in her diary as "frightful & painfully and disagreeably human."

Say the ape, the Eurasian magpie, or the elephant looks in the mirror and recognizes the paint smeared on her body by the researcher. The animal who passes the mirror test then investigates her own body for the offending mark. Say she finds nothing. How long before she trusts the reflection over her own body? Say the mark on her reflection is confirmed by all the other elephants. How long before her reflection replaces herself? Say the mark is not of paint but instead a word applied to her.

"I got my period when I was ten, and I'd been reading Judy Blume books for a while so I knew it was coming," said Tanaïs. "And when it came, I wasn't prepared for it anymore." A 2011 American Association of University Women (AAUW) school survey shows that early development is the most common attribute of sexually harassed students, followed closely by perceived prettiness.

"You sort of feel alien in your own skin and ashamed for existing," said another woman I interviewed. "Being a busty eleven-year-old was difficult," said another. "My breasts were a burden to me. I felt ashamed of them because of the constant comments and attention they got from everyone of all ages."

"In my cultural milieu of Bangladeshi people living in America," explains Tanaïs, "being light-skinned and slender and straight as a fucking arrow is beautiful . . . I knew very early on: I'm not a light-skinned, skinny, fuckin' straight-as-an-arrow bitch. I'm not that person at all." She goes on, "I had very thick Coke-bottle glasses, braces, hairy upper lip and legs, acne, *and* an adolescent, emerging voluptuous body—my face didn't change until four or so years later."

Most of the literature on this topic, including a 2009 *Social Psychology Quarterly* article, "The Double Standard and Adolescent Peer Acceptance," finds that "the term 'slut' is typically applied by females to other females whose bodies or behaviors deviate from group norms. Exotic beauty or premature physical development may then be enough to threaten the status quo and result in a girl's exclusion from female peer groups."

" 'Shame' is the word I keep coming back to," Tanaïs, who is strikingly beautiful, continues. "The way that my body developed did make me feel shame in that space . . . I felt undesired by all, since South Asians were considered ugly and unfuckable, and I suspected a list circulating about the ugliest girls in middle school included me." She adds, "In '90s heroin-chic white hegemonic beauty standards America—without Black women and Bollywood (even with its light-skinnedness) I'm not sure I'd ever come to find my beauty."

Leora Tanenbaum, the author of two books about slut-shaming, adds, " 'Slut' serves as an all-purpose insult for any female outsider. All the social distinctions that make a teenage girl 'other' are collapsed into a sexual distinction." I interviewed twenty-two women who'd experienced this kind of sexual harassment before writing this essay, and nearly all of them qualified during adolescence as some kind of "other," whether it was a designation earned by race, body shape, economic class, gender presentation, or family background.

There was another way to be collapsed into a sexual distinction, though. Now I can see the perfect trap of it, how the solution to feeling disgusting would become the proof to all that I was.

It was the first real hot day of summer, the summer before I turned twelve, and we were watching boys play basketball in Kimmy's driveway. There was Ty, a pretty-faced sixteen-year-old with tennis-ball biceps, and three of Kimmy's brothers. My hair stuck to the back of my neck, and the cars were too hot to lean against. Down the potholed street, a mirage shimmered, a puddle of heat.

They were huge, these boys. They smelled of Old Spice and menthol cigarettes. There was anger pushing up inside them; I could hear it in their clipped voices, feel it in the sharpness of their gazes. Their bodies, even in graceful motion, were always fighting. Their limbs swung and flew, threads of sweat tumbling off them. They were louder when we watched. When they glanced at us, I shimmered like that mirage at the end of the street. Their attention quickened me, turned me into something lithe and bright—less body than flash of light. What a relief it was.

When an older guy sauntered up and one of the boys yelled his name, Vega, I lurched in recognition. When I was younger, my father would lift me onto his shoulders and teach me the names of stars. One arm wrapped around my shin, the other pointing up, he'd breathe their strange sounds into the dark: *Sirius, Polaris, Arcturus, Vega.* In summer, Vega could always be found above the top of our street, flickering its changing colors. That was its atmosphere shifting, my father had told me. It became my favorite star, this celestial body that was always becoming a different kind of beautiful. This Vega in Kimmy's driveway was kind of beautiful, too, with his tiny mustache and golden arms. He was, in the way of men and space, both unfathomable and familiar.

"This one's for you," Ty said with a wink, and wove his way through the grunting clot of bodies to sink the ball through the hoop. Kimmy screamed. She had fallen on a tree branch, and a piece of wood the thickness of a finger had lodged itself into her thigh. She wailed, suddenly a child. Her brother carried her into a car, and someone drove them to the hospital. I managed to get left behind.

"In body dysmorphic disorder," writes Thomas Fuchs in a 2003 *Journal of Phenomenological Psychology* article, "the patient is overwhelmed by the others' perspective on himself, while feeling his own self-devaluation in their gazes." Living inside my body had already become a fraught existence. If I were going to be defined by the gaze of other people, why wouldn't I step toward the ones that made me feel beautiful? I didn't know yet how temporary that feeling was. "Since this devaluating (self-)perception, as we saw, is corporealizing at the same time, it prepares the ground for a reified body perception . . . The vicious circle of corporealization and shameful self-awareness has become fixed. The 'body-for-others' now dominates the lived-body."

Wanted was the only thing I was sure I ought to be. There it was, bright in the eyes of every boy in that driveway. A reflection of me that bore a different mark—at least, it felt different—and I wanted to feel another kind of different.

Vega carried two cans out of the kitchen and handed me one. He seemed so comfortable in Kimmy's house, as if it were his own.

"Here, mamacita." Milwaukee's Best, it read. I set mine down on the carpet by my foot. I had only ever tasted the foam from my father's occasional Dos Equis. I perched on the edge of the couch and sucked in my belly. Vega sat beside me. MTV was on and a man and woman rolled around on the beach, sand stuck to their bodies. He took a long drink from his can, then balanced it on the arm of the couch, the muscles of his back shifting through his white T-shirt. It was new; I could make out the creases from its fold inside the plastic package. A black tattoo crept out of the sleeve and down his arm. He was handsome, with sharp features and long eyelashes, but at least twenty-five, a grown man.

On the TV a woman stood beside a poster of a fatter version of herself. She kicked the picture away from her and marched toward me, holding her arms out to display her new skinny body.

"So, you got a boyfriend?" Vega asked.

"No," I said.

"Oh yeah? You ever date a Puerto Rican boy?"

"No," I told him, "but my dad is Puerto Rican."

"Oh yeah?" he says. "So you are a little mamacita, huh?"

I was unfamiliar with the term, and though I didn't speak Spanish, I knew enough to parse out its literal meaning. If it had been my abuela who had said it, maybe after she taught me to cook plátanos maduros fritos, I would have glowed with pride. But in the mouth of this strange man, I knew it meant something different. I smiled nervously in agreement, because he seemed so pleased and I wanted to please him so badly, this strange grown man, without knowing why. His tone was thick with knowing, and I understood that he recognized something in me.

I didn't know then that *mamacita* is different from *mamita*, that though the literal translation is also *little mother,* "the moniker is never really used to describe an actual mother," as Laura Martinez wrote in a 2014 op-ed for NPR. She explains that the term is "inextricably linked to a man's perception of a woman as an object of sexual desire." Which is to say that it communicates a desire to impregnate a girl—to make her into a mother—more than any sense of diminutive endearment.

I was not a little mother or a hot mama. I was an eleven-year-old girl. Now, it seems to me a startlingly efficient way to age a child in a single word. Sometimes the word itself matters less than the authority with which it is spoken. It is the act of naming that claims you.

When I walked across the room toward the bathroom, my sneakers sank into the carpet like it was sand. I closed the door, but the lock was broken. I peed, running the faucet to hide the sound. After washing my hands, I leaned toward the mirror to inspect my face.

When the door opened, I was surprised and not surprised at the same time. He slid his body into the narrow space behind me, and I hunched forward, as if to let him pass. He didn't pass. My hips pressed against the sink. Afraid to see his face in the mirror, I looked down at the shape of my breasts under my T-shirt. I could feel the outline of his body, its heat an image reflected on me.

He leaned down and kissed the side of my neck. Hot breath against my skin, his face in my hair, huge hands clasped around my waist, fingers pressed into the bare skin above the belt of my jeans. My breath came shallow, like it did when I was afraid. I was afraid. The empty house around was suddenly vast, as if we were flung into space. Vega's stubbly cheek grazed the back of my neck, and his hands slid upward.

A car door thunked outside. I raised my eyes, and they met his in the mirror. It felt like bursting up out of water, into light. I could move suddenly, and I did, clasping my chest. I felt his fingers shift beneath my hands, and even with the fabric of my shirt between us, his felt as if they were inside of me, a part of my own body.

"I am suddenly caught," explains Fuchs, "as it were, in a force field, in a suction that attracts me, or in a stream that floods me. I am torn out of the centrality of my lived-body and become an object inside another world. The other's gaze decentralizes my world."

Here is a story: around other girls I was fat and misfit, condemned by some inherent flaw in my body's constitution. Here is another story: around men I was desirable, possessed of a flickering power that I did not know how to control. Here is another story: when Kimmy got back from the hospital, she asked why I hadn't come. *You stayed here?* she said. *By your-self?* I told her Vega had stayed, too. Her face twisted, and I flushed with shame. Or did I flush with shame and then she made a face? In any case, we built it together: a story that wasn't true, but which we both believed. Eventually, she told it to others. Here is another story: around my family I was messy and loved. Then I was a liar. I was possessed by a power they did not know how to control.

My body seemed to literally transform, depending on what eyes beheld it, like a superhero or a monster. Years later I would feel it when I went home, all those child selves clamoring back into being. I would itch to get away and return to my adult life, so that my body could morph back with each mile's distance.

The specular self does not stay in the mirror, of course. Fuchs explains, "The mirror represents the perspective of the others on my body: by taking over this perspective on myself,

self-consciousness is constituted. An essential step in this process is marked by the development of shame."

The story of the self will be written no longer by the child's anticipation, or what she knows as inevitable in the *Innenwelt*. It will be written by the birthday girl with the greased chin. It will be written by the men whose hands mold her into being. It will be written by the mother and the father and the neighbor and the magazine and all who stand to benefit from claiming her. In Lacan's words: "This moment at which the mirror stage comes to an end inaugurates . . . the dialectic that will henceforth link the I to socially elaborated situations."

The self becomes a collaboration with other people, a series of fantasies that lead to "the armour of an alienating identity." Have you seen a suit of armor? There are so many pieces. Here is where a strange man named me. Here is where the girls stared. Here is the school report card. The plates clink and move together like one. The self underneath is invisible to others. We are completely alone inside ourselves.

"Once grasped by the other's gaze," Fuchs writes, "the lived-body has changed fundamentally: from now on, it bears the imprint of the other; it has become body-for-others, i.e., object, thing, naked body." It is a cliché that adolescents care too much what their peers think, more sobering to think of the power we give to others at that age. Not *Like me*, but *Conjure me*.

"She's tight," they kept saying with glee about this girl or that. This was before tight meant good or mad and after it meant drunk or cheap.

"What about me?" Is it possible that I actually asked this? That I was once so plaintive? Of course. I was a child.

"No, you're loose as a goose."

I remember exactly what I wore that day: button-fly jeans, short-sleeved shirt with a floral pattern. It must have seemed important. I must have looked down to see what they saw. There was no red mark, but that didn't mean it wasn't there.

The geese in our town shat everywhere. Their long black necks were fat as the pipes under our kitchen sink, their sleek heads identical, with white-feathered cheeks. Their wingspan was enormous. Sometimes they flew in a V formation, their muscular wings beating in unison, their bodies' improbable masses gliding over us in an arrow, honking as they sliced into the sky.

I did not feel loose as a goose in the bathroom with Vega. I did not feel loose as a goose later that summer, with Kimmy's cousin in the kitchen. I did not feel loose as a goose with my other friend's brother in the closet, or another friend's brother's friend behind the mall after school.

I felt loose as a goose alone in my bedroom, my magnificent wings beating the air, flapping the pages of all my books.

Still, I let them touch me. It seemed that my desire and theirs ought to be connected, that what drew together ought to have some shared reward, though it never did in practice. My desire found its dead end in them, and there was no easy route out.

I recently reread Edith Wharton's *The House of Mirth* and found it almost too painful to finish. I had not remembered that it was a novel about dying of a bad reputation. I only remembered that Lily Bart was beautiful, that she becomes addicted to "chloral," and that such a fate seemed either likely or appealing to me.

I loved tragic stories of smart women whose difference led to ruin. Better yet if they were also beautiful. The romance of tragedy was a balm I could apply to my own sorrows. I felt different in so many ways, not least of which in the way I looked—not blond and freckled like the most popular kids, but tan and green-eyed, with the body of a woman. I had always been told I was exotic—*what are you?*—but it had started to feel like an insult.

"This is how to spit up in the air if you feel like it, and this is how to move quick so that it doesn't fall on you," the speaker of "Girl" teaches her daughter—I always imagine by wordless example. You can be loose as a goose so long as you make sure that no one sees you.

I have never felt sympathy for the mother voice of the Kincaid story until now. "The slut you are bent on becoming" is not a sexually promiscuous woman. The mother doesn't think her daughter is bent on sleeping around. The slut is what she will become if people call her one, if she does not manage her reputation. To be called a slut is tantamount to being one, she tells her daughter. Society creates you. They already want to believe this about you; in some way, they already do. Don't give them confirmation.

A woman must cultivate a double self: the public self and the real self. Somehow, you must keep that fragmented self, no matter if Lacan tells you it's impossible. Your life depends on its management. You can dream and think and spit and fuck as long as you don't keep a sloppy house. As long as you don't leave fingerprints or pennies in the bread. If you do, that's it. They can do anything they want to you.

I had heard that *Easy A* was a feminist teen movie about slut-shaming. In the 2010 film Olive (played by Emma Stone) is a virgin, a smart student who is moved by the plight of Hester Prynne in Hawthorne's *The Scarlet Letter*, which her English class is reading. On a whim in the girl's restroom at their high school, Olive lies to her best friend that she's lost her virginity to an older guy in community college. The lie is overheard, and the rumor mill churns. Soon everyone knows about the imaginary community college student, and Olive (sort of) enjoys the increased social visibility. Subtlety is not one of *Easy A*'s strengths, though it needn't be—the double bind that insists that teen girls exhibit performative sexuality and then ostracizes them for doing so is not subtle either.

"There were rumors started about me that I sucked dick, that I, you know, liked to get it from behind, all this stuff," Tanaïs tells me about the time after she was raped by her first boyfriend, and subsequently became sexually active. "And it was perpetuated by young women too, it wasn't just young men, it was younger women . . . I remember my chemistry teacher was like, 'There's really ugly things being said about you in the girls' bathroom, do you want us to get rid of it?'" Instead, she decided to check it out first. "They spelled my name right, which I was like, really, really impressed by." She laughs. "I was like, okay, this is my entire name, no confusing who the fuck it could be, and I was like, 'You know what? Just leave it.' And I wore it as this weird badge of honor.

"I would rather be this bitch that's talked about and people are kind of jealous of, obviously, than to be someone who's in pain and trauma and suffering because of this thing that happened to me," Tanaïs elaborates, with a shrug. "Even though I would cry a lot about feeling really lost and not being able to share with my parents or even my younger sister what I'd gone through, or even friends, or anybody really."

When a gay classmate begs Olive to pretend that she's had sex with him, too, to refute the truer rumors about his sexuality, she agrees. They pretend to have sex at a party where all their classmates overhear. Soon her best friend feels compelled to tell her that their classmates are referring to her as a "cum dumpster."

"Do you think I'm a cum dumpster?" Olive asks.

"If the dumpster fits," her friend replies. Soon Olive is dressing the part, in a bustier and full face of makeup, a scarlet letter affixed to her chest.

Tiffany was not a close friend, more of a school friend, and it would likely have been the only sleepover we ever had anyway.

The smells of other people's houses sometimes allured me in their novelty, but the too-sweet smell of Tiffany's house made me instantly homesick.

Tiffany's older brother was more interesting than either Tiffany or her ruffled bedroom. When she introduced us, I felt burnished by his attention, the kind I'd already become an expert at detecting. I could feel a man's gaze when it heavied with interest, like the birds who flitted at the feeder in our yard could feel mine. Desire filled my bones with air. Tiffany noticed, too. Later, when she suggested we play Truth or Dare, she dared me to ask him to join us. Then she dared us to go in the closet. There he kissed me, probing the inside of my mouth with his tongue. As the dresses shifted on their hangers in the dark, I recognized the mix of fear and excitement that fizzed in me. The same sense, when he touched me, that I no longer existed. Not girl, but vapor. My body a thing in his hands, my mind a balloon bumping the closet ceiling.

On Monday, I was summoned to the principal's office and arrived to find Tiffany waiting there, a tissue clenched in her hand, I was confused. She told the vice principal that I was going to get a bad reputation. She thought I ought to be punished for her hurt feelings. She felt used, she said. I did not think to apply the same word to myself. I did not feel wronged by her brother, though it had not exactly felt like a choice. When the vice principal suggested that I apologize to Tiffany, I did, my face burning, without knowing exactly for what.

Ray is a twenty-six-year-old PhD student at an Ivy League university. A Brooklyn native, she describes her seventh-grade self as having "uneven bangs and braces and bruises all over my body from skateboarding and climbing trees." Athletic and academically gifted, Ray mostly made friends with boys her own age. "I was very aware that I couldn't really confide in my female friends," she explains. "It felt like anything I said could be used against me and that I was someone other girls wanted to take down."

One night during seventh grade, upon the request of a boy she skateboarded with, who went to a different school, she recorded a video of herself masturbating and sent it to him in exchange for a dick pic. By the next day, she was receiving questions from other kids on AOL Instant Messenger: Did she really send out a video of her pussy? "Some boys sent me messages saying they had seen it," she tells me, "asking if we could come up with an arrangement of sorts."

She was sitting in class when the seventh-grade dean walked in and shouted her name. He walked her to his office in silence. There, he referenced the video that had circulated. "He didn't ask me whether or not it was true," she explains, "he didn't really ask me what my side of the story was, but seemed to have accepted that I had sent a video of my dirty pussy to some kid he didn't even know . . . because I was a slut." She shrugs. "He shamed me in ways I can't really put words to."

In *The House of Mirth*, Lily Bart's mother also teaches her daughter that society's regard is everything. That "a beauty needs more tact than the possessor of an average set of features." That she must manipulate and manage both her gifts and society's esteem to get what she needs, to be safe. It makes sense that Lily is always looking in mirrors; she knows very well that the specular self is the social self, the one on which her life depends.

But there are two Lilys: the one ravenous for approval and security, who believes entirely in "the great gilt cage in which they were all huddled," and another, more private one. When she disobeys society's rules, the rules of her mother, in that grace period before the other inhabitants of the cage begin to punish her for her transgressions, she can feel it, "one drawing deep breaths of freedom and exhilaration, the other gasping for air in a little black prison-house of fears."

First, it was just the other students in my class, kids I'd known since first grade. I was loose as a goose, I was easy and fast, mostly because of the way I looked. It only took a few true stories to stoke that fire.

One night I was eating dinner with my family, and the phone rang. A tiny bolt of lightning struck in my chest, and I leapt up to answer the call. "Don't answer that," said my father. "No phone calls during dinner." I ignored him and snatched the phone from its cradle in the next room. There was a shuffling at the other end of the line and then a gravelly girl's voice shouted, "You're a fucking whore!" into my ear. At first I wasn't sure if the voice had filled our whole house, or just me. Had my parents heard? They hadn't. I fixed my face and went back to dinner.

That first time it happened, I wondered if I should have apologized more sincerely to Tiffany.

It is Gus Trenor's wife, Judy, who is Lily's best friend early in the book. It is she who warns Lily, in her pursuit of a potential husband, about the dangers of being perceived as "what his mother would call fast—oh, well, you know what I mean. Don't wear your scarlet crepe-de-chine for dinner, and don't smoke if you can help it, Lily dear!"

Lily doesn't marry that man, and she doesn't fuck Judy Trenor's husband, but she does accept something she needs from him: money. That is enough.

Olive doesn't accept money from the other nerds whose reputations she agrees to rehabilitate at the cost of her own, but she does accept gift cards, preferably from the Gap, Amazon, or OfficeMax. Soon her best friend joins the high school Christian clique to picket outside the school with enormous signs proclaiming that Olive is a whore.

The most frequent caller, she of the gravelly voice, was Jenny, a sophomore at the high school. One day after school, Jenny's older boyfriend and his friends had noticed me. Their attention, like all of that from older boys, dazzled me like headlights on a dark road. I froze, exhilarated and scared. Nothing physical had happened between Jenny's boyfriend and me—just an exchange of light. That was enough.

I became the mistress of the telephone. No one got to it faster. I came directly home after school and parked myself next to the beige contraption with its long, curly cord. It was not always Jenny—sometimes other voices told me I was a slut and described the ways they were going to punish me for it—but I came to know that gravelly voice. I only saw her face once or twice from a distance, but I thought of her more than any boy, more than any friend I no longer trusted, more than anyone but myself.

Only the boys made gestures. Why should that one be imprinted in my memory so deeply? My memory, so often a bag of muddy cloth, and this stone hardly rounded by time. The skinny boy fingers, splayed around his mouth, the leering eyes.

The tongue is the only muscle in the human body that is only connected to bone at one end. It is the only muscle that never tires. It is relentless, wagging luridly at me across twenty-five years.

There were times that we exchanged more than light. Every one of them, I got burned. They were all a version of that afternoon with Vega, but often less lucky, less interrupted—a different boy, a different bathroom, a different place beneath my clothes. Every time, I was that mirage, or they were. I was gone. I was sorry before it ended, hot with regret by the time I got home. I already knew the story, knew that I was helping to build it with the kindling of my own body.

They told us to say no to so many things in school, but never how. My father insisted that boys were not to be trusted under any circumstances. My parents encouraged me to respect my body, to protect it. But what did that mean? For better and worse, I've rarely been capable of summoning respect simply because I was told to. Sometimes the things I did felt like a kind of protection.

"In that moment," Ray says of her meeting with the seventh-grade dean, "I believed in my disembodiment, I believed that I wasn't the sum of my parts, I believed that some of my parts weren't mine, they were for sharing with horny boys on the internet. I also believed that I was smart. And smarter than the horny boys, and smarter than the idiot seventh-grade dean."

I believe that she was, too, but her intelligence couldn't stop the dean from bringing a petition around to all the seventh- and eighth-grade classrooms regarding whether Ray had sent the video. An eighth-grade girl told Ray that the dean had made everyone sign it and that at least a hundred kids had. "I think she also told me she had signed it," Ray remembers.

The part of me that knew how to climb trees and disagree with my teachers, who drew "deep breaths of freedom and exhilaration" without thinking, she was not gone. She felt gone, though. The other one, the one "gasping for air in a little black prison-house of fears," her dark smoke had obscured every-thing else.

I had not been a fearful child. Now I was afraid to go to school. I was terrified of Jenny, of the violence she might do to my body. I was terrified of my body, how it had gotten me into such trouble. I was terrified of my family discovering how reviled I had become. I would protect them from the punish-ment my body had earned.

Here's the thing: they were already calling me a slut. Before they ever said the word. Before I let any boy touch me. Like the mirror-tested animals, they saw the mark on me, and though I didn't see it, I came to believe it was there. In hindsight, it makes sense of the shame every girl feels at this kind of bullying. It's not that we are ashamed at being humili-ated but that the story of us has been revised to include the thing that warrants humiliation. Even when we know it's not true, or at least not right, a part of us believes it. To tell my mother that they called me a slut would have been to reveal that I was one.

For months, Trenor insists that Lily pay him special attention. She avoids him, but he will not be placated. In their final, terrifying encounter, he sends her an invitation under the guise of his wife's name. Lily arrives at his door that evening to find that his wife is not even in town. His whining swells to menace. He feels owed, not only because "the man who pays for the dinner is generally allowed to have a seat at table," but simply because he wants her. As Lily rebuffs him and tries to leave, the careful manners that govern the world inside their gilded cage evaporate from him like steam. How quickly his desire, when thwarted, turns to hatred. It is on this grave miscalculation of Lily's that the whole book, and her life, turns.

Though she does not pay that debt with her body, she pays it with her reputation, which often amounts to the same in the end. Whatever power she has held depends entirely on the esteem of others, and once that falters, it becomes clear to both Lily and the reader that he can do anything he wants to her.

Olive's degradation reaches its nadir when, in the midst of her ostracization, a boy at school asks her out on a date. Unbelievably, she accepts. After a pleasant dinner, they stroll through the restaurant's parking lot, and the boy hands her a $500 gift card to Home Depot. Olive's face falls. Resignedly assuming he wants the same ruse as the others, she asks him what supposedly transpired on their so-called date.

"Whatever five hundred dollars gets me," he answers, and forcibly kisses her.

We barely knew each other, Jake and I, had hardly ever spoken. He was the older brother of a classmate I'd known since elementary school. What he thought he knew about me was enough. In the busy hallway of school, he stopped directly in front of me, so I stopped, too. He reached out a hand and roughly groped my breast through my shirt, his gaze steady on my face. I froze. He withdrew his hand, smirked, and walked away. I had no idea if anyone had seen. In twenty-five years, I have never spoken of it aloud, though I have thought many times how lucky I was to be confronted by him in a school hallway and not behind a closed door, at someone's home, after a few beers.

I was terrified of that gesture—the gruesome tongue tucked between two fingers. A part of me will never stop being shocked by it, by the ease and cruelty with which those boys conjured my twelve-year-old genitals. The concept of my sexual pleasure had become an obscenity, a mean joke delivered for their own amusement. I'm sure they could not have clarified their meaning, were simply exhilarated at their new power, but I understood: they could claim that part of me in any spirit they wanted, in the school hallway with unwashed hands, as a joke between them, as an act of humiliation or violence.

We had known each other since we were little kids. I had helped them with their homework. I had seen them pee in their pants and cry in school, been to their birthday parties, and watched their mothers wipe their faces. Loyalty, I began to understand then, can rarely be taken for granted.

Like Ray, I knew that I was smarter than them and could still beat most of them in a fight. You don't have to recognize power for it to be wielded over you, it turns out. And what power they suddenly wielded over me, what willingness to use it as a hammer.

When the first social outcast asks Olive to cosign the lie of their intimacy in exchange for payment, she refuses. The nerd sputters that he doesn't need her permission, visibly elated and terrified by the realization that he could do it anyway. They both understand that Olive is already compromised, her word so quickly devalued by her alleged sexual activity that any boy's is worth more.

When Lily contrives to escape the brewing social hell that her contract with Gus Trenor has inspired, she goes on a cruise with a longtime frenemy: Bertha Dorset. When Bertha is caught cheating on her husband, she deftly obscures her own wrong by accusing Lily of sleeping with him. Whatever resurrection of her name our heroine hopes to nurture is quickly dashed.

"What is truth?" she asks. "Where a woman is concerned, it's the story that's easiest to believe. In this case it's a great deal easier to believe Bertha Dorset's story than mine, because she has a big house and an opera box, and it's convenient to be on good terms with her."

That is, everyone knows it unlikely and unfair, but everyone signs the petition anyway.

We were studying some aspect of American history, discussing a true rumor about some dead president, when my teacher said, "The thing about reputations is that they are usually true."

There it was: my reluctant sense of fairness, my feeling of being wronged. It bloomed in me like a corpse flower, rare and putrid. I was afraid to be angry. If I let myself get angry, I would have to face my own sense of the injustice, the true breadth of my own powerlessness. There are benefits to believing what they say about you.

Did I argue with him? Probably not, though I knew he was wrong. Not only on behalf of my own bad reputation. What is a reputation but the story most often told about a person? Perhaps the bad stories told about white men throughout history have mostly been true. After all, the threat of punishment for telling false stories about white men has often been great. Likewise, the ability of white men to correct the record. But the stories those men tell about women, queers, or anyone who is not white? Power is required to inflict punishment and to revise the public record. You need a weapon to defend your own name. If you don't have one, they can say anything they want about you.

I don't think my teacher meant that reputations are usually true in the Lacanian sense of a self that is built by social collaboration. He meant that if they say you're a slut, you're probably a slut. Which implies that a slut is a kind of woman, rather than a word used to control women's bodies.

In 1487 a Dominican monk in Germany, Heinrich Kramer, published the treatise *Malleus Maleficarum* on the tail of a bill that allowed men to prosecute witches as heretics. Kramer—like most men of the church, from the Christian Fathers to his contemporaries—was obsessed with the sexual purity and inferiority of women, though his obsession reached such demented extremes that he was eventually exiled. Women, he thought, were lower even than other animals, as Eve was an unfinished animal. Witchcraft was the result of their insatiable desires, Kramer argued, and the most common culprits were those "hot to fulfill their corrupt lusts, such as adulteresses, fornicators, and the mistresses of rich and powerful men." The result? They fucked demons, stole men's penises, ate babies and made ointments out of their pulverized bodies. It was a rationale for and guide to the persecution of witches—the greatest threat to society, the church, and men that history had ever seen.

Before he wrote the *Malleus*, Kramer asked for the arrests and torture of fifty women who he accused of witchcraft, including those who had reputations for being independent or free with their views or who disagreed with him publicly. Kramer was so obsessed with the sexual practices of one such woman that his local bishop expelled him and suspended the trial. No matter, he wrote the *Malleus*, which became a bestseller for two hundred years, surpassed only by the Bible.

Sometimes I think of the men who bemoan their ruined reputations after women come forward to expose the ways in which they have been abused or mistreated by these men. The men seem shocked by the consequences, which is unsurprising, as men have been allowed to abuse and mistreat women for centuries without consequence.

I think of their lawsuits, their indignant editorials, their secret votes, the other men who must murmur sympathy to them in private, balls shrunk with the fear that they will be next to face consequences for their actions, how they cry that it's *a witch hunt!*

Sometimes I think of these men, and I think *ha!* Mostly I don't find it funny at all.

The thing about *Easy A* is that we are allowed to be aghast at Olive's treatment because it isn't "true." However alone our heroine feels, the viewer is always there to witness her "innocence." She is not alone in the truth of herself. Whereas we who were punished for the things we did or didn't do, we were alone. There was no one to confirm the truth of us. There was not even a way to speak it.

However feminist in its intention, the premise the movie takes for granted is that a slut is a thing you can be, and that you get to be one by having consensual sex. Sure, all the horrific holy-roller high schoolers come off badly, but the movie never challenges the idea that a girl ought to be pure and manage her reputation to avoid being ostracized and raped. I would have liked the movie immeasurably better if, instead of being about a beautiful, smart virgin who acquired an unearned reputation and then cleared her name and bagged the super-nice boyfriend, it was a movie about a girl who actually had extremely hot sex with her queer best friend and then fucked a bunch of nerds for Home Depot gift cards and was still presented as a sympathetic protagonist.

I am still waiting for the movie that tells us that nothing a woman can do or wear earns her that kind of treatment, that presents the concept of a slut as the battering ram it is, used to keep women isolated from their own pleasure, their true selves, and one another, and to prevent them from challenging any aspect of male domination.

Just think of all the things that could get a woman called a witch. Which is to say, all the things that could get a woman killed: having opinions, being poor, being rich, having female friends, not having female friends, disagreeing with a female friend, refusing to testify that another woman is a witch, disagreeing with a man, looking askance at a man, not having sex with a man, having sex with a man, a man's impotence, being very old, being very young, being a healer, being a slave, having no children, having too few children, being stubborn, being strange, being smart, being beautiful, being ugly, having spoiled milk in your home, floating, having a mole or a wart or even a swollen clitoris that might be interpreted as a telltale third teat, meant to suckle your familiar.

The most common way to kill a witch in Europe was to burn her; in New England it was hanging. But there was also crushing, drowning, and beheading. Torture that didn't draw blood was not even considered torture.

It is a brilliant legal trajectory. Invent the witch who is a threat to your religion and everyone's souls. Make witchcraft illegal and put men in charge of trying the accused. Make the woman a beast of low morals and perverse passions. Make any behavior that threatens you a sign of witchcraft. This way you can punish her for anything. You can make her humanity monstrous. Now you can do anything you want to her. You are the hammer of sorceresses.

Not everyone believed the wild misogynistic tales of Kramer's *Malleus*, but plenty did. What was it but a story about women?

In the video that I show my students of Jamaica Kincaid reading her short story "Girl," the laughter of the audience when she reads the line "the slut you are so bent on becoming" is disturbing because nothing about her story or its reading is funny. The laughter of the audience is disturbing, also, because it is the laughter of a white audience, and Kincaid is a Black woman.

"Black women sometimes experience discrimination in ways similar to white women's experiences; sometimes they share very similar experiences with Black men," writes Kimberlé Crenshaw, who coined the term *intersectionality.* "Yet often they experience double-discrimination—the combined effects of practices which discriminate on the basis of race, and on the basis of sex. And sometimes, they experience discrimination as Black women—not the sum of race and sex discrimination, but as Black women." Every time I have examined an aspect of discrimination on the basis of sex, it has led me back to this fact: whenever systems of oppression intersect, their power compounds—those of sexism and racism in particular. Because my essays arise from my own experiences, which do not sit at that intersection, I rarely follow it to any substantive depth beyond recognition. (There are copious writers doing brilliant work on the subject, some of which are mentioned in this book's bibliography.) On the subject of slut-shaming, however, it arose so often in my interviews with other women and in my reading on this subject that it seemed important to do more than simply recognize or refer to that experience.

"The two names I was called in seventh grade were slut and nigger," Mira tells me. "It was always white children who called me these words." Like all the women of color I interviewed, Mira acknowledged the intersections of her experiences with racism and slut-shaming. Now a forty-two-year-old high school teacher, she grew up middle-class in a small city in Southern California. "I was one of the few Mexican students on campus," she says, "and I think that my racial 'othering' was what precipitated the slut-shaming."

Though in seventh grade she did not even know what sex was, Mira found herself "constantly sexually harassed and assaulted by white classmates. They grabbed my butt, thighs, crotch and breasts and did so in front of male teachers . . . [who] chuckled or blushed and looked the other way." The physical molestations led to further harassment. "When boys would grab me sexually," she tells me, "they would hiss the word 'nigger' into my face."

"I always think about Halloween, my senior year of high school," says Aja, a forty-year-old Black woman and former college classmate of mine who now lives in Oakland, California, where she was raised. During high school Aja attended an elite East Coast boarding school where she was one of few students of color and even fewer Black students. "There was a faculty-judged costume contest in the dining hall . . . I dressed up as Jem, from Jem and the Holograms.

A cartoon I'd watched as a kid. Lots of makeup, side pony-tail, shiny clothes, short skirt. I overheard the judges confer-encing on who they would cut first. 'So obviously the hooker has to go, and who else?' I was confused at first. There was no one in a hooker costume. Then I realized it was me. I was the hooker.

"I wonder," she continues, "if I hadn't been black, would they have been able to imagine that I was a kid dressed up as a cartoon character? But honestly, the wondering is over-stated. I know. I have been a black woman long enough now to know. Black people are criminal. Painted women are promis-cuous. Ergo, black painted woman = criminal sexuality. Hooker. It would be surprising in America if they didn't go there."

"In the United States," the feminist group Black Women's Blueprint's "Open Letter from Black Women to the SlutWalk" (2011) reads, "where slavery constructed Black female sexu-alities, Jim Crow kidnappings, rape and lynchings, gender misrepresentations, and more recently, where the Black female immigrant struggles combine, 'slut' has different associations for Black women."

SlutWalk was an action organized by Canadian feminists after a Toronto cop quipped during a routine safety lecture that "women should avoid dressing like sluts in order not to be victimized." After the first march in Toronto, SlutWalks spread across the United States, and then Argentina, Australia, the Netherlands, New Zealand, Sweden, and the UK.

Black women in the United States balked at the SlutWalk's supposed reclamation of the word because, in the words of the "Open Letter," "it is tied to institutionalized ideology about our bodies as sexualized objects of property, as spectacles of sexuality and deviant sexual desire. It is tied to notions about our clothed or unclothed bodies as unable to be raped whether on the auction block, in the fields or on living room television screens."

While she was an undergraduate at the liberal arts college where we met, Aja had "an older Trinidadian boyfriend who was violent, and raped [her] at least twice." She confided in a professor, who accompanied her to the precinct of the neighborhood in which the rape happened to report it and to file a restraining order. "The officer who took the report was perfunctory and even seemed annoyed," Aja remembers. "Until I mentioned my attacker was on parole and in violation." At that, the officer's eyes visibly lit up. "He got some other cops and ushered me into a paddy wagon. He was gonna use me as sting bait," she explains. "They did not give a shit that I was raped. They gave a shit about their collar. Like every goddamn thing a black man does is criminal in their eyes except raping a black woman."

If a slut is a thing a white woman can become because anyone decides it, then what of a Black woman, whose innocence and purity have never been invented by white men to protect or rescind? In the history of this country, she has already been deemed unrapable. The story of her sexuality has already been written to justify her complete disempowerment, to erase her humanity.

Likewise the woman indigenous to any colonized land, the transwoman, the inmate, the refugee, the undocumented immigrant. In addition to her femaleness, each aspect of identity that moves a woman further from white heterosexual manhood increases the impact of discrimination against her, the justification for men of doing anything they want to her.

Living two lives distorts the temporal experience. Misery dilates time. It only lasted a year, but that was a forever. At school, I was harassed. At home, I became angry and sullen. On the weekends I sought relief in the gaze of men, though their hands always left me empty. Like Vega, their colors were ineffable, always changing. We look up at stars and like the way their light falls on us, but if you try to touch a star it will burn you to nothing. I burned with self-hatred, as if I'd ingested a poison that was slowly blackening my insides.

Some Buddhists believe in hungry ghosts. When a person dies and is consigned to this role, the experience that follows is considered a milder version of hell. The hungry ghost might have an enormous belly and a long, needle-thin neck. Invisible during daylight, she roams the night, ravenous. Maybe the food turns to flames in her mouth. Maybe she can only eat corpses. Maybe her mouth itself has gone putrid. In any case, she can never satisfy her hunger. She is always disappointed and she is never full.

I longed to be the Lily who "had at last arrived at an understanding with herself: had made a pact with her rebellious impulses, and achieved a uniform system of self-government, under which all vagrant tendencies were either held captive or forced into the service of the state."

But that was not even Lily, in the end. We were both of us hungry ghosts.

"That year was the same year I started snorting coke and drinking alone while I showered and stealing my mom's painkillers," Ray tells me. "It was the same year as so many events I cannot or will not recall in this moment." After it, her reputation as a slut "wasn't something people questioned." A friend asked her for a hand job on his birthday, and she gave it. "He told everyone," she reports. "I didn't really care. I was so unattached to myself and to my reputation that one more dick didn't mean anything."

Flash forward two years or so, and she "was sitting in a psychiatrist's office at a lockdown boarding school in the middle of nowhere. I'd taken at least three or four HIV tests since I'd been in rehabs and institutions." The psychiatrist explained that even though she had gotten multiple negative tests back, "there was still a chance I was positive. He explained that my promiscuity put me at high risk. He left our meeting saying something to the effect of, 'Bet you wouldn't have slept around like that if you knew this then.'"

"My mother calls those my 'sexy girl' years," Ray says. "But I didn't orgasm with male partners until I was in college. Sex with men, beginning at age twelve, always felt mechanical. I dissociated and tried to stay as far away as I could. Even when I started sleeping with women, also around age twelve, I felt like I had to put my partners' desires first. I was the disembodied fragment of my seventh-grade pussy on the internet."

In her book *Fearless Wives and Frightened Shrews: The Construction of the Witch in Early Modern Germany*, Sigrid

Brauner writes, the *Malleus Maleficaram* develops "a powerful gender-specific theory of witchcraft based on a hierarchical and dualistic view of the world . . . Perfection is defined not as the integration or preservation of opposites, but rather as the extermination of the negative element in a polar pair. Because women are the negative counterpart to men, they corrupt male perfection through witchcraft and must be destroyed."

It was hard to know which half of myself to destroy. The versions of me that other people saw and created: the slut, the sullen daughter, the outsider; or the other one, who read until her eyes crossed and mind burned with ideas, who loved the power and possibility of her own young body, who glimpsed the cage of society and its open door? To have faith in the latter was tempting, but a risk. She was so capable of being hurt.

I tried to hide, to starve, to gorge, to detach, to escape, to deny, but nothing worked for any length of time. Some days, I knew that the only way to find relief would be to destroy them both, and that, I already knew how to do.

In 2016, researchers at the Centers for Disease Control and Prevention published a data analysis that showed suicide rates rising 200 percent among girls age ten to fourteen between 1999 and 2014.

If I were to reiterate even a portion of the documented cases of adolescent girls who killed themselves over bad reputations, many of which occurred after they were assaulted, I would have to make this essay a book. Thankfully, such books have already been written.

When I imagine there having been an internet, social media, or smartphones when I was an adolescent, the future—my present—goes hazy. It's tempting to believe in my own underlying integrity at that age, to believe that I would have prevailed even then to whatever extent I have, but in truth I suspect I might not have survived at all.

Lily doesn't want to die; she just wants to sleep. Her life, now one of poverty and isolation, offers that only relief. She is so tormented by the events that led to her ruin that the opiate sleeping draught is her lone route to "the gradual cessation of the inner throb, the soft approach of passiveness, as though an invisible hand made magic passes over her in the darkness."

I would also have found it "delicious to lean over and look down into the dim abysses of unconsciousness," to "[wonder]

languidly what had made [me] feel so uneasy and excited."
But I did not find my chloral for a few more years, and that
was lucky, because otherwise my story would have ended the
same as Lily's.

It is how the story of the slut almost always ends. Sometimes she is exiled, like Little Em'ly in *David Copperfield* or
Hester Prynne. Rarely is she redeemed—in *Easy A*, her sex
is a farce and her virginity intact, thus she emerges unscathed.
Mostly, the slut dies. The trope of the murdered slut in horror
movies is so familiar that it has a name: "Death by Sex." By
contrast, only one woman is ever allowed to survive a typical
horror movie: the "Final Girl," who must be as pure as her
dead friends are dirty.

Daisy Miller dies of Roman fever. Nana Coupeau dies of
smallpox. Ophelia dies by drowning herself. Tess Durbeyfield
dies by execution. Emma Bovary dies by swallowing arsenic.
Anna Karenina dies by throwing herself under a train.

I did not die.

3

At the time, I would have said that even worse had happened:
my father read my diary. Though I didn't have words then to
describe what had been happening to me, I did keep a detailed

log of my sexual interactions. Even now, twenty-five years later, I blanch inside to imagine him reading that unannotated inventory. I have never been more humiliated and relieved at once.

My parents sent me to the only private school in our town for seventh grade. Nothing was very different there, except me, in new ways. At the private school, the girls got professional manicures, lived in homes with four bathrooms, and vacationed in Europe.

Only a few of us at the private school were unrich enough to take the chartered school bus, and I quickly became familiar with the small handful of others. A ninth-grade boy with whom I struck up a friendly acquaintance said to me one day, "You're the only oversexed seventh-grader." He didn't mean to be cruel, said it like a fact we both already knew. He might have thrown a rock at me, it struck so hard.

What did he know of me? Only what he could see: my body. Maybe the way I had learned how to inhabit it. That I, like him, was different from the other students. I wanted to tell him that I was a virgin, as if this technical qualification would prove his assumption wrong. What did oversexed even mean—that I had too much sex or that I wanted too much sex? I wanted to tear him apart like the maenad he thought I was. I wanted to cry. Instead, I laughed and looked out the bus window.

All the way through *The House of Mirth*, I just want Lily to stop playing along. To step outside the mirror and keep walking. The other self inside her is clearly loose as a goose, ready to sprawl across the sky vaulted over the frilly dinner tables at which she suffers. She *sees* it, more clearly than I could at thirteen.

"How alluring the world outside the cage appeared to Lily, as she heard its door clang on her! In reality, as she knew, the door never clanged: it stood always open; but most of the captives were like flies in a bottle, and having once flown in, could never regain their freedom."

I find myself thinking, How could she? Though I have known for a long time that while freedom requires knowing, knowing does not guarantee freedom. The ability to see that the door is open does not render us able to step through it—perhaps that is the most torturous part, and those who can see most clearly the most tortured people.

It is not only that Lily believes in the self that society sees, or in society itself, but also that she is alone. There is no other set of eyes to sew her back together, to confirm the truth of her *Innenwelt*. Despite all of her annoying materialism, the agency she never assumes, the terrible choices and wasted privilege, it is one of the loneliest stories I have ever read.

The worst and most lasting part of that time was how completely alone I felt. This is the brilliance of shame as a tactic of domination: it conditions us to maintain our own isolation. The genius of a social structure is that you cannot see it; it is built to be invisible to you, this machine that compels you to perpetuate it. But I was not alone. None of us were, or are.

When I returned to public school for eighth grade, a classmate told me, "You should meet Jessica. She's like you." I still don't know what he meant exactly. That she was called a slut, like me? That she had a secret self inside herself? That she listened to different music than the rest of our classmates and dressed in thrift-store T-shirts? All of those things were true. We recognized each other at first sight. From then on, she became a different kind of mirror, one that I desperately needed.

Jessica and I both had messy rooms and hair. We both got good grades and hated school. We both had deadbeat birth fathers and premature boobs. Soon we had a list of running jokes long enough to last the whole school day and a habit of talking on the phone until we fell asleep. We listened to Nirvana and never talked about what we had done with any boys.

Sometimes they still called us sluts, and then they called us lesbians. The difference between being called a slut alone and being called a slut or a lesbian with your best friend cannot be overstated. "So what," we said, and laughed. "If we weren't such good friends," we said, "we would absolutely be sleeping together."

Lily only feels the freedom of her Real self in those rare moments when she is around the person who cosigns its reality. Then "gradually the captive's gasps grew fainter, or the other paid less heed to them: the horizon expanded, the air grew stronger, and the free spirit quivered for flight. She could not herself have explained the sense of buoyancy which seemed to lift and swing her above the sun-suffused world at her feet."

When my parents sent me to Unitarian summer camp, I imagined that it would be a tour of compulsory activities as boring as they were wholesome: hiking and campfires and trust falls into the arms of teens who swore they'd never let a cigarette soil their lips. If I had known then about the sex education program that Unitarians offer their youth—in the Our Whole Lives (OWL) program, they definitely talk about female orgasms—I would have known to expect different.

To my great surprise, this camp offered workshops like "existential crises on the back porch," zine making, and creative writing led by a Nick Cave look-alike named Dave, who gave us Rilke's *Letters to a Young Poet* and said only one sentence all afternoon: "I hate white people," even though camp was mostly attended by white people.

The camp director that year was a woman named Nadia. In her early twenties, Nadia was six feet tall in combat boots and overalls, with a shaved head and arms emblazoned with tattoos. She stomped rather than walked and used the word *fuck* as though it were the interstitial glue that held all other words together.

I hadn't known that women like her existed, that her kind of beautiful was an option. When she looked down at me, I felt more seen than I'd ever felt under another person's gaze. I have since learned that recognizing the invisible parts of oneself in another person can feel like a radiant kind of love. It can make those parts stronger inside you.

"I remember the queer kids," Tanaïs recollects, "mostly in my drama and art class vibes, that was another avenue in which I could just be my slutty self and hook up with people and not even be a judgment. It was just like, I'm hooking up with people. And those people were mostly white, I will say, white queer people who were open. I never really thought of those people as the white girls, they were my gay white friends and they were separate for me. Even today, in my heart"—she laughs—"my closest white friends are all queer people."

After three weeks at camp, I understood a lot of things that I hadn't before, including that being good friends does not preclude being lovers. Within days of my return, Jessica and I kissed. Her mouth was so soft! I'd never touched a breast not my own. Hers were different, smaller, nipples the color of Band-Aids instead of dark like mine. I did not empty of myself. I was not left with any oily after-feeling. This, too, was a knowledge that grew the world and what I understood as possible in it.

On the weekends, I made a queer feminist zine that I copied at my local library and distributed all over town. Every hand-cut issue I left—in a napkin holder at the diner, on the tables in the school library, under the windshield wipers of cars on Main Street—was like picking back up a piece of myself. Even when one of my teachers pulled me aside after class and suggested I might be suffering from mental health issues, I did not waver. The self inside me had been recognized. Nothing could undo that, not the boys who said that being bisexual made me a slut or even the dissolution of my friendship with Jessica, six months after it became sexual. I was flying the cage, however long it took.

"Thank god we had that voice that allowed us to emerge out of these shitty downs and these stupid family dynamics and cultural dynamics that try to steal your power and your love for yourself," says Tanaïs. "I'm really grateful to her, that fourteen-year-old, for being who she was."

The summer after eighth grade, a year after my return to public school, I worked as a maid for a roadside motel in town. There, one of my coworkers was an older girl who it took me a few shifts to recognize: Jenny, my most frequent prank caller. She still had that gravelly voice, smoked menthols, and used a lot of hair spray, but there were stretch marks on her belly and dark shadows around her eyes. There, both of us sluts in the oldest sense of the word, we became a kind of friends. We traded complaints about filthy guests and shared her cigarettes while we waited for the washing machines to complete their cycles. We both remembered those calls she made to my home, each of us breathing into the strange darkness of the other, but we never spoke of it, because while there were so many words for what back then, there weren't yet any for why.

There is a part of me that still can't bear to see it in other women—*the slut you are bent on becoming*—that shimmer, that man-sourcing of self, that vaporous need to please, to fill the invisible belly with the thing they told us was food. It hurts to look at them, and even I feel a twinge of that muddy desire: to punish them, to prevent them, to protect them.

I suspect that as long as a part of me hates them, it is the persisting part of me that hates my young self, that is still afraid of being the girl in the mirror. Or even the less young self, who sought attention as if playing the slots, handed herself over for the impossible chance that it might pay off in some lasting way. She didn't get punished the way I had as a kid for entering that mean lottery, but she did go broke in other ways.

I can't undo the years of my life I spent marked. When you leave the cage, you take the mirror with you. It took a bunch more years for me to smash it.

"I forgive myself for ingesting shame I did not choose but was fed anyway," says Aja. "I may not yet be unashamed, but I am wholly unapologetic."

My story is an ordinary one. All of ours are. Many worse iterations of it are playing out right now and will continue to until we all understand that *slut* is a word that men invented, like *witch*, to maintain power over women and to keep them in service to men. Hatred and fear of female sexuality is baked into the foundation of civilization as we know it, and sluts are most often women who threaten the colonial regimes of patriarchy and white supremacy.

It turns out that almost everything they will call you a slut for being is a thing I want to be. I am finally loose as a goose, my wingspan unfolded its full length, my powerful neck raised as I slice into the sky. I am the same woman in the *Innenwelt* and the *Umwelt*. I am that careless girl, hands sunk haphazardly into the dough, bedroom a sty, pen stilled against her hand, eyes cast out the window, mouth humming a song, thinking of something else. I am that outspoken witch; I will disagree with any man. I am a firework gone off in the dark, a spectacle of disobedience, a grand finale of orgasms anytime I want.

I don't want to take the word *slut* back, like I don't want to own a gun. It was never mine. You'll never hear me say it to any woman, not as a joke, not with pride or affection or irony.

The only definition of the word that I claim is the one of a rag dipped in lard and set afire. Call me that kind of a slut. Call me flashlight. Carry me through the dark if it helps. Here, take this story and watch it burn.

WILD AMERICA

NARRATOR: You're a girl, not an animal.

VALERIE: A she-mammal or a female child. I was on the
borderline between human being and chaos.

—Sara Stridsberg, *Valerie*

Eloise Brill and I sat on the beach at Goodwill Pond while
nearby our fellow campers ate cellophane-wrapped sand-
wiches on rotting picnic tables. It was the summer of 1989,
and our parents had enrolled us in afternoon swim camp at
the public pond. Rumor among the elementary school set was
that the water in Goodwill Pond was warm and yellow because
of not sunshine and pollen but rather a high concentration of
pee. It seemed plausible, given that we all definitely peed in
the water. I didn't care. I had just won the afternoon's timed
race and was buoyant with my victory.

"Are you a lesbian?" Eloise asked me, smug as only a nine-
year-old with a new word can be.

"I don't know," I said. "What's a lesbian?"

"Give me your hand," she said. When I did, she pressed
hers against mine, the grit of sand between our sticky palms.

Someone's happy scream bounced across the water, followed by a splash. Eloise squinted at the tops of our fingers. "See?" she said. "Your ring finger is longer than your pointer finger. That means you're a lesbian."

I drew back my hand to examine it. She was right. What else might my body reveal about me that even I didn't know? The thought crept through me like a shadow. I shrugged. "Let's go eat lunch," I said and brushed off my hand on my swimsuit, as if I could leave the worry there in the cool sand.

Consider the Hecatoncheires. Three children of Uranus and Gaea, they were named for their hundred hands. Cottus, the striker; Gyges, the big-limbed; and Briareus, the sea-goat, maker of storms. They were giants who grew up to defeat the Titans. They were earthquakes and sea storms, powerful beyond measure.

Now, consider the Hecatoncheires before all of that. Not as triumphant warriors, not as the guardians of Tartarus. At the beginning. What is a sea storm as a child? How does an earthquake begin to know itself? That first rumble you hear and think: *me*. Our power may be innate, but we learn its meaning from others. No one is born knowing the difference between a sea god and a sea monster. What if no one told you that you were a Hecatoncheire? Where would you hide all those hands? How could you not start to hate them?

Before I learned about beauty, I delighted in my body. I was a passionate child with callused feet and lots of words. I talked fast and moved faster—through the woods around our Cape Cod home, up trees, and into the ocean's crashing surf. Finely tuned to the swells of my own and others' hearts, I sensed a deep well at my center, a kind of umbilical cord that linked me to a roiling infinity of knowledge and pathos that underlay the trivia of our daily lives. Its channel was not always open, and what opened it was not always predictable: often songs and poems, a shaft of late-afternoon light, an unexpected pool of memory, the coo of doves at dusk whose knell ached my own throat and seemed the cry of loneliness itself. It was often possible to open the channel by will, an option that I found both terrifying and irresistible. I would read or think or feel myself into a brimming state—not joy or sorrow, but some apex of their intersection, the raw matter from which each was made—then lie with my back to the ground, body vibrating, heart thudding, mind foaming, thrilled and afraid that I might combust, might simply die of feeling too much.

Though this state seemed obviously the most *real* and potent form of consciousness, I knew that it was not "reality." Later, this understanding evolved into a fear of my own susceptibility to madness, but as a child I simply understood that a person could not live with an open channel to the sublime inside them; it was impossible to hold on to the collective story of human life with that live cord writhing through you, showering sparks like a downed wire in a hurricane. Human life was defined by composure and linearity, school bus routes and homework and gender and bedtimes and taxes. Though I could meet its requirements most of the time, I knew my adherence to the logic of reality was tenuous, that a more feral sensibility reigned beneath it.

The resiliency and strength of my young body was a source of comfort in the face of this dissonance between inner and outer worlds, because it offered a link between them. The body was a weird unfathomable masterpiece, a perfect shard of what coursed through that channel. My body was not, however, subject to radical shifts in consciousness. It was always *real*. It always felt good to know that I could easily climb the enormous oak tree beside our driveway, swim to the center of our pond, exert a concrete power on the physical world with my own two hands. Indeed, my hands seemed the locus of my body's ability, their pliant strength leading every physical encounter, their size—larger than most other children's—a measurable proof of substantiality and of a creative intelligence far beyond the human.

The game was this: alone, I would trudge to that place in the woods where the pines were tallest and, at the right time of year, the ground a bed of their smooth needles. Close to our house but not in view of any human construct, I would lie on the ground, close my eyes, and clean my mind like a chalkboard. Sometimes I made a story for myself, but it was crude and beside the point: I was from another planet, I had been struck amnesiac—all that mattered was that I'd fallen from the sky a stranger. My eyes would flutter open and carefully absorb my surroundings. I might clutch a handful of pine needles to my face, inhale their green scent, touch a slender spoke to my tongue. In summer I would wade into the pond, imagine it was the first water ever to close around my ankles like two cool mouths.

In the outskirts of our yard, I stalked our family dog, my heart pounding. I discovered the garden hose and drank the contents of its sun-warmed belly. Sometimes I made it all the way inside the house without detection. Oh, the frightful pleasure of making the most known place in the world an alien landscape. The cool shadows of an interior. The naked smoothness of floors. The absurd bounty of cabinets stuffed with food. My wonder was bottomless for the world empty of stories, mine alone to name.

"The higher the animal, the more it plays," *Wild America* host Marty Stouffer explained in one episode. "Once the demands of instinct, such as the need for food or sleep, have been satisfied, animals have the time and inclination to play." *Wild America* was a half-hour show that aired on PBS from 1982 to 1994, created by Stouffer, a native Arkansan and nature conservationist. Each episode began with its triumphant horn-laden theme and an introduction by Stouffer himself, clad in a colorful sweater and groomed beard.

"True play is aimless, with no goal other than to experience new sensations," he elaborated. Nonetheless, he went on to explain, often play is also constructive. Young mountain goats strengthen their legs by leaping and romping mere minutes after they are born. Juvenile martens stalk squirrels in a pageant of the hunting techniques they will use as adults. "I think we can learn something from this," Stouffer mused in his voiceover. "Perhaps we could find a way to play less desperately, and to learn more playfully."

I loved *Wild America* not for Marty Stouffer's philosophical digressions but because, like my game in the woods, it reset the context of the familiar. However often Stouffer imposed human narratives on the animals depicted (very often), it was still always clear that survival was the priority that assigned value to everything in the animal world. If the wild marten was overcome by her own feelings, she didn't let it stop her from procuring dinner for her babies. I might have had to close my eyes during the part of the nature documentary when the pack of hyenas felled an antelope, but they had no qualms about tearing warm mouthfuls from her while she still kicked with frantic life.

My mother had raised me vegetarian, and though I harbored no real desire to eat meat, sometimes, in summer, I would take a hunk of watermelon to a remote corner of our yard and pretend it was a fresh carcass. On all fours, I would bury my face in the sweet red fruit-meat and tear away mouthfuls. Sometimes I'd rip handfuls out and cram them between my teeth, which wasn't much like any animal I knew of. It was less playing a particular kind of animal than enacting a form of wildness that I recognized in myself but that had no appropriate expression in human culture.

I watched *Wild America*, along with the more savage nature specials on public television, and thought, Maybe. Maybe no one else recognized themselves in the hyena's blood-soaked grin, her ruthless hunger. Maybe no one else's heart raced, fists clenched, neck tensed—unable to tell if she was more impala or lion. Well, I did. Alone in the woods behind our house I had beaten my chest, acted out my own invented stories without a thought to how another's gaze might see me. I sympathized with the jittery business of squirrels and fanatical obsessions of our golden retriever. I was confounded by silverware, why it should exist when we had such perfect instruments at the ends of our arms.

Walt Whitman claimed our distinction from animals to be that "they do not sweat and whine about their condition," and "not one is dissatisfied, not one is demented with the mania of owning things." I learned in elementary school that we were animals, but unlike other animals, we did not seem driven by the instinct for physical survival. We were so far up the food chain that it was no longer even visible to us. We were beyond survival, in a dark and lofty realm wherein our obsolete instincts had been perverted into atrocities like capitalism and bikini waxing. I might not have been able to name this, but I recognized it.

Sometimes, when I momentarily detached from the narrative of human life that we all took for granted—the one that presumes that money, cars, shopping malls, pollution, and all of industry are not a catastrophic misuse of our resources—and glimpsed it from a more evolutionary angle, it seemed so bizarre as to be unlikely. Was this life or some strange dystopian movie, a dream we were all having and from which we would soon wake to resume our sensible animal lives, in which "nature" was not a category of television show or a variety of experience to cultivate a preference for consuming, but the only thing, the everything?

In elementary school, however, we kids were not making an ontological study of late-twentieth-century middle-class American life. We were neither learning about capitalism nor reading Whitman. We were learning how to *be* human. We were learning the exact way in which, though we were animals, we should not look or act like them. To call someone an animal was an insult. As my peers and I approached puberty, this was unfortunate, because I had trouble keeping track of the narrative. I was covered in scabs and bruises. I was sun-browned, full of sighs, and interested in every orifice. I was an animal.

By middle school, this felt like an especially disgusting secret, because I was also a girl.

Sometimes I think about going back. I imagine reversing the film of my personhood, reeling the spool to find the single frame where it all changes. As though there would be one murky celluloid square in which my body was taken away from me. Not just my body, but all the pleasures that came through it. A hand reaching into the frame and snatching it all away—the sting of salt water on my skinned knees, the ache of a palm tendered by oak bark, the pelt of gravel against my calves as my bike flew downhill, the hum of my legs after running all day, my own voice ringing in that cathedral of pine trees, the perfect freedom of caring only about what my body could do and never about how it was seen.

There wouldn't be just one frame, of course. It was so many things. The skinny girls splashed all over movie screens. The television set my mother tried to keep out of our house. The slippery issues of *Teen Magazine* that started arriving in our mailbox. That classmate at her pool party, silently commenting on my precociously developed figure. The rich girl who pinched my thigh and pointed out how much thicker it was than her own.

I didn't learn to hate my hands until the end of fourth grade, when my body exploded—almost a year after Eloise Brill and I sat on the beach at Goodwill Pond. It was mutiny, flesh swelling from my chest and thighs before it did in anyone else my age. I was enormous, I thought, Alice after eating the wrong pill, busting through the house of what a girl should be. I was the Incredible Hulk, but instead of a superpower, my size and strength were a damnation. Girls were not supposed to be enormous. They were not supposed to be scabby and strong. Inexplicably, strong and big were what every animal wanted except us.

To be human meant that unlike in most other species, females were the cultivators of meticulous plumage. We competed to be the weakest and smallest and most infantile. We seemed to spend all of our resources withering ourselves to be attractive to males. The goal was to be as soft and tidy and delicate as possible. It made no sense at all. I was not in the habit of withering myself. I was not tidy or delicate.

I had always eaten the same way I did everything—with speed and vigor. One day at lunch, after I polished off a soggy square of cafeteria pizza, the girl next to me stared with bald observation.

"What?" I said, self-consciousness radiating through me.

"You eat so fast," she said with a touch of self-satisfaction. "I can't even finish a whole piece of that. It's so *big*."

Wild America had taught me that wolves could go more than a week without eating, but I could only make it one day. *I won't eat anything but string cheese this week*, I promised myself. One Saturday, the only thing I consumed was a bag of sugar-free Jell-O powder. I licked my fingertip and dipped it into the tiny bag of red sand until it glowed crimson, until my mouth was aflame with chemicals, as though I had poisoned myself. I would have poisoned myself if I thought it would transform me into a smaller animal.

In hindsight, the extreme reversal of values—big and strong going from best to worst—shocks me. Men seemed to have it all, to be considered superior in all perceivable ways, and yet we were discouraged from striving for any form of dominance deemed masculine. To be described in any way as "manly" was the vilest of insults. Such adaptability was required of us to perform this internal U-turn, to conform our loyalties to this crackpot framework, rife with contradiction. I can see now that our ability to do so was evidence not of a lacking survival instinct but of a finely tuned one. What I needed to survive middle school just happened to be the opposite of what I would have needed to survive on *Wild America*.

Instead of eating contests, we had starving contests. Instead of boasting of our strengths, we forged friendships by denigrating ourselves. Instead of arm-wrestling each other, we compared the size of our arms, competing not for strength and size but puniness. It didn't take long for someone to point out that I had "man hands," an insult I subsequently used to abase myself well into adulthood.

I inherited a lot from my mother, though I first recognized my hands. We have long fingers, wide palms, and strong nails.

They don't carry our ring sizes at mall kiosks. We shop for gloves in the men's section of department stores. We don't bother with bangle bracelets. In adolescence, it struck me as unfair because my mother was beautiful, with fine features and dizzying cheekbones. No one was ever going to be distracted from her face by her hands. But me? My hands gave me away. I was a Hecatoncheire among humans. My two miracles had become monsters.

In school, I learned to talk less. I moved slower and hid my body in oversize clothes. I longed to be a smaller and cooler thing, less wanting, less everything. Though I felt gigantic, I wasn't. It was not the first time I mistook the feeling for the object, and not the last. This is what happens when you give your body away, or when it gets taken from you. Its physical form becomes impossible to see because your own eyes are no longer the expert. Your body is no longer a body but a perceived distance from what a body should be, a condition of never being correct, because being is incorrect. Virtue lies only in the interminable act of erasing yourself.

My body, though fickle in conception, was starvable, concealable, subject to the reconfiguration of desire—when someone thought it pretty, so it became. Not my hands. No matter how my self-conception changed from moment to moment, my hands remained long and strong and wide and scarred. They were maps that led to the truth of me. I was no petaled thing. I was not a ballerina. I was a third baseman. I was a puller, a pusher, a runner, a climber, a swimmer, a grabber, a sniffer, a taster, a throw-my-head-back laugher. I used my hands—they were marked by things and left marks. They would never let me become the kind of girl I had learned I should be.

What of the girl I actually was, the one who rose from a bed of pine needles to name her own world? She was exiled. The channel that connected the wild in me with the wild outside could not be destroyed, but I did my best to seal it, as I strove to tame my own nature and wither my form. I turned away from the real inside of me and oriented myself outward. I did not look back for a long time.

What we hate or fear most in ourselves tends to be among the things we first notice in others. As anorexics read cookbooks, I started to read hands. They reveal us all, it turns out. Even our fingerprints are the evidence of how we touch. First, when we are three-month-old fetuses, our fingertips' skin outgrows its outer layers, buckles under the swiftness of change. Then we form their ridges by grasping the walls of our mothers' wombs and our own bodies, feeling our way through that first small world. In this way, that world shapes us, defines our physical selves more permanently, more individually, than any part of this greater one.

As a teenager, I learned to mute a person's words and watch their hands. Chewed cuticles, jagged or polished nails, knuckles lumped with scars—the motion of a person's hands often mimics the motion of her thoughts. Hands grope for elusive ideas and clench the ones we want to hide. They flutter like propellers, moving us closer to the right words. They pinch and squeeze to police us, the silent gestapo of our inhibitions.

My hands were undisguisable, so I learned to hide them in my pockets and sleeves, behind my back, under my thighs, and in fists—my two anemones, closed in the perpetual nighttime of shame.

By the time I was thirteen, I had divorced my body. Like a bitter divorced parent, I accepted that our collaboration was mandatory. I needed her and hated her all the more for it. Despite my deep sympathy for all other animals, I was sociopathic in my cruelty toward this one. When she disobeyed me—in her hunger, in her clumsiness—I was punitive and withholding. I scrutinized and criticized and denigrated her ceaselessly, even in dreams. Not before or since have I felt such animosity toward another being.

There were moments, though. As a teenager, at night, alone in my bedroom, sometimes the illusion of autonomy from my body would crumble and I would be flooded by the most profound sorrow and tenderness. I would look at my strong legs, each scar on my knees a memory. My soft little belly that had absorbed so much hate. Even my hands—like two loyal dogs that no amount of cruelty would banish. I suddenly saw my body as I would any animal that had been so mistreated. My poor body. My precious body. How had I let her be treated this way? My body was *me*. To hate my own body was to suffer from an autoimmune disease of the mind. In these moments I had the thought that I was mentally ill—in a literal sense, for what else could describe this hostile relationship to my very own body? I had no way to differentiate what aspects of my behavior were inherently *me* and what were cultural impositions—insofar as this task is ever possible. What I could see clearly was the violence with which I treated the body that held custody of those other ineffable aspects that I considered to be myself. It held me, and I ought to have held it with equal care. I was unspeakably remorseful, as I imagine any abuser would be in such a moment of self-appraisal. I sat in the dark and hugged myself. "I'm sorry," I whispered and squeezed my own shoulder. "I love you," I said. While I slept, the veil would draw once more. In the morning, I rose from my bed and looked in the mirror with disdain: *You again.*

Now those moments seem proof that self-love is an instinct, as animal as any other function of the self. The ferocity of my affection could not be erased, only suppressed under total vigilance. My self-hatred was not self-generated. It was an expression of the environment outside of my body, which, it eventually turned out, I could change.

My first girlfriend, Lillian, confused me. Her short, matted hair and carpenter's pants. The duct tape that sealed the rips in her down coat. Her soft voice and easy tears. Her delicate hands that rustled thoughtlessly in her pockets or against my face. Even paint-flecked, with perpetual crescents of dirt under her nails, she was more girl in this way. I wanted to kiss her all the time. I also envied her the freedom of that ethereal form. In it, she could be herself and still be beautiful. What did I think would happen if I did the same? I'd be seen an ogre, all my hundred hands exposed.

For most of my sixteenth year I spent most of my free time with her, which was a considerable amount, as I'd dropped out of high school. I might have been self-possessed enough to insist upon homeschooling myself, but I was consumed by insecurity around the one person whose esteem I desperately sought. Whatever power they had held over me and however they had shaped my thinking, by fifteen I saw my former classmates and teachers as irrelevant, characters with walk-on parts that would never appear again in the story of my life, whereas I needed Lillian to *love* me, and that meant I had to scrupulously hide the aspects of myself that I suspected might repel her. This was sheer projection—Lillian may well have been attracted to me *for* those very qualities—I simply had no reference but the most base heterosexual model of how to be attractive to another human.

I spent the majority of my time in her company tense with control. My body was bigger than hers in so many ways, and I feared drawing attention to this fact by being too flagrant in my movements, my laughter, my opinions. I had successfully internalized the belief that all my animal aspects—including, and perhaps most of all, the inherent vigor with which I approached life itself—were an affront to my femininity and should be annihilated if possible, and, failing that, vigilantly suppressed and camouflaged. My experiences in school had taught me to hate my body, to mute any protruding aspects of myself that might draw attention, but my relationship with Lillian refined this skill. With her, I could be openly queer. I wore men's shirts and battered Doc Martens. I didn't wear makeup, but I was still in disguise. A fascistic watchfulness governed my body.

After observing us together, a friend of my mother's once commented that I seemed "so much more mature" than

Lillian. It was true that there was something childlike in the way my girlfriend inhabited her body. She sat with her legs either akimbo or improbably knotted, fidgeted restlessly, ate with her hands, and regularly stared into space for whole minutes. I found her seeming lack of self-consciousness mesmerizing and worshipped it as yet another corporeal ideal unattainable to me, a freedom that could be afforded only by those more finely constructed. That is, because she was beautiful, she could be uninhibited, even slovenly. I was young enough to still suffer from the misapprehension of beauty as freedom, the idea that if a woman succeeded by the impossible terms of patriarchy she might graduate in some way from its hold. For years I longed to affect this appealing tension between elegance and dishevelment. My mother's friend could not have been more wrong, I thought, in her assessment of the difference between Lillian and me. Nevertheless, I met her error with an uneasy mixture of relief, pride, and anguish—an experience that would become familiar in the years that followed, and likely is to any truly secretive person. It was proof that my fastidious efforts to conceal both my real self, whatever that was, and my profound insecurity were working. I was again alone in the truth of myself, but this time under my own direction.

But how to indulge any genuine impulse in this landscape of control and obfuscation? My desire for Lillian was *real*.

We'd kiss for hours in her messy bedroom, stopping only to flip the cassette tape or gulp a glass of water. My desire was a galloping thing, and her touch, unlike that of boys, didn't snuff it out. If my body had been a passive machine from which men made withdrawals, like an ATM whose code they were handed on the day of their first erection, then with her it was a winning slot machine, screaming jangly music and spewing coins.

Sexual pleasure was equally thrilling and terrifying, not for the usual reasons. We had not gotten far beyond heavy make-out sessions, and though I longed for more, I did not dare. My desire was a portal, the single permitted link to my wild and true self that Lillian had access to. I lived in fear that were I sufficiently possessed by lust, I might expose too much of myself and drive her away. I was well enough versed in the scripts for female desire to know that we were supposed to have it, or at least perform it, but in a girlish, mewling way. My desire was not that. Like the right poem or song or slant of light, it was a doorway that opened directly into the part of me that understood hyenas better than humans. I sensed that there was a threshold over which I would completely lose the ability to monitor myself. Like a power surge or septic tank failure, I might flood the room with my putrid worst: make guttural noises, contort myself in grotesque positions, reveal the bestial facts of me.

I was cautious in our exertions, rarely daring to touch her in some way she had not already touched me. After hours of kissing and groping, my hips would rock with frustration. What next? We didn't have the internet then. We didn't know what else to do. We weren't brave enough to try something. Which one of us was the boy? I wondered. I was terrified and certain that it would turn out to be me.

One day we lay on a blanket in the grass of her backyard. The trees hummed with insects, the air was hazy with pollen. I read a novel, peering over it occasionally to watch her dip a paintbrush in a slick of watercolor and drag it along her sketchpad, the wet tip like a tiny black tongue, streaking the white with purple.

Eventually she tore out the paper and handed it to me.

"For you," she said and kissed the top of my head.

I took the paper, suddenly buoyant with hope. I had not known enough to want this, but still, it had found me. For a moment, anything seemed possible. Even my own happiness.

I smiled at her and then turned to study my gift. Next to the colorful figure of a woman's nude form and a tree with tangled branches she had painted a short poem.

"Sometimes you touch me more like a bear than a butterfly," read one line. Shame shot through me in hot streaks. Me, with my clumsy bear paws. *Wild America* had long ago taught me that a bear needs her enormous paws for climbing, swimming, swiping, and navigating landscapes of ice—what good were mine? I felt ugly and crude, prehistoric in my proportions. I felt like Lennie in Steinbeck's *Of Mice and Men*: crippled by my own hands, misfit for human society, terrified of crushing the things most precious to me.

It's a lesbian cliché—the first-date hand comparison, not so widely known as the U-Haul joke, but a hallmark of every romance I've ever had with a woman. Straight people do it, too, but the interaction doesn't hold quite the same charge because men and women don't primarily fuck each other with their hands.

In my twenties I started announcing "I have really big hands" whenever I saw the moment coming. "So do I," my dates often replied, but mine were always bigger. My fingers stretched longer and my palms wider that those of women six inches taller than me. The rest of me was muscular and curved but concealable, mitigated by my petite stature and the heels I wore every single day. I had spent decades disguising the rest of my body with sartorial modifications, but my hands were brazenly big, unabashedly big. There was no getting around them.

If I had been fucking my lovers more, I would have gotten over it faster, and if I didn't hate my hands, I surely would have been fucking my lovers more. The women I loved dressed in men's clothes, were always taller and bigger than me in most ways. And mostly, they fucked me. From the moment I began really having sex with women, I was grateful to be queer, to realize that my attraction to my partners had nothing to do with their adherence to oppressive definitions of femininity. Lillian remains the only female lover I've had with whom I confused wanting and wanting to *be* in that particular configuration; the opposite was true of all my subsequent paramours—my attraction to them had nothing to do with that old idea of beauty as delicacy. I cherished the spread of their thighs across chairs and their weight on top of me, inhaled their musky scents with relish. I craved the animal in them. Nevertheless, to offer myself the same freedom was still inconceivable.

Though I recognized the gift of a sexual experience so much less bound by heterosexual prescription, I was not free. No lover had ever seen me naked with the lights on. I never forgot myself. Whenever a lover looked at me, so did I, fastidiously monitoring the position of my limbs and torso lest they give away their secret enormity. I still feared what my body might reveal before I could.

It wasn't that I rationally *thought* any of them would stop loving me if I stopped striving for an ideal I'd settled on at twelve years old. It was a belief and a set of behaviors so deeply implanted in me that it resided beneath my intellectual functioning. I had "known" better for years. Knowing that we've been conditioned doesn't undo it. I had surveilled myself for two decades, nurtured the fear that if I didn't, I'd expose some hideous corporeal reality that would repel those whose affections I most craved. I couldn't just decide to stop, nor had I. I lived then, as many women do, like a house inhabited by dueling caretakers. One always papering the walls for some anticipated guest, the other tearing them down. One cooking elaborate meals just for the other to throw them in the trash. Imagine the energetic waste! Probably you don't have to, because you know yourself the way one can build a life around fighting the patriarchy and still have parts of your own mind believe that your worth correlates exactly to your desirability to men. Consciousness doesn't preclude false consciousness. It is one of feminism's raisons d'être.

This imbalance in sex worried me, though I never spoke of it. I don't believe, and didn't then, that all sex ought to be perfectly reciprocal. But I knew that ours wasn't, in part, because I was afraid. I was afraid that if I fucked a lover, she wouldn't like it, or that I wouldn't. I was afraid that I *would* like it and find myself repulsive. Worse, that she would find me repulsive. I was still afraid of being the boy.

In her essay "Uses of the Erotic: The Erotic as Power," Audre Lorde defines the erotic as "a resource within each of us that lies in a deeply female and spiritual plane, firmly rooted in the power of our unexpressed or unrecognized feeling." Our oppression, she claims, is predicated on the suppression of this resource and its inherent power; "As women we have come to distrust that power which rises from our deepest and nonrational knowledge." I had read Lorde's essay in college and loved it, without comprehending the full breadth of its relevance to my own life. A mercy, because I was not yet ready to change. When I read it again, I was ready.

In my early thirties, I became conscious of the fact that I had been in consecutive monogamous relationships since my teenage years. It was notable, I thought, but also fairly ordinary. Lots of people were always in relationships. I was just a relationship person, I told myself, though even in the privacy of my own mind it had the ring of rationalization.

"Don't you think you should take a break?" my mother asked me when I was thirty-two. I had just ended a three-year domestic partnership.

"Probably," I said, though I had already begun the next one. When it ended, I decided that I really ought to take a break. I wanted a different kind of relationship and knew that it was me who needed to change. Then I got into four or five much shorter consecutive relationships. By thirty-five, I understood that the decision to take a break could not be a casual one. Too much of me for too long had been oriented toward other people and their attraction to me. A break would only be possible if I drew a solid line between not only myself and those most overt entanglements of sex and love but all the precursory activities as well. There could be no flirtation, no friendship even partially predicated on sexual tension, no voyeuristic perusal of dating apps. I was a person so habitually attuned to the charge of attraction that I *accidentally* got into committed partnerships.

Since middle school, when I rejected the power and pleasure of my body as a sublime vehicle and traded it for the framework insisted upon by the rest of world, I had considered the value of my body primarily as it related to other people, namely men. By my thirties, though I rarely saw men as potential partners, that framework still defined much of my experience. A part of me still loathed my physical self—hated my big hands, thought my proportions cartoonish and grotesque—and that part of me found the transformative power of others' desire an irresistible relief. Being in a relationship provided a constant source of this relief, while reinforcing my habitual reliance on others' perceptions of me as a condition of self-acceptance.

It was hard, at first. I had to restart a few times, so rote was my behavior. But when I truly committed to the quest of being alone and of turning inward, the change was immediate. Like a plant growing toward the sun, my life began to open. Or something began to open in me that let more of life in. My time was suddenly my own, which subtly but completely changed the texture of beingness. I ran and slept and taught my students and talked for hours on the phone to my friends and family. For the most part, these were the same things I had previously done, but they *felt* different, as if I had taken off a pair of gloves that I hadn't known I was wearing. I reread "Uses of the Erotic," in which Lorde explains that "the erotic is not a question only of what we do; it is a question of how acutely and fully we can feel in the doing," and sighed with recognition.

I wrote all day, until I wasn't sure if I even remembered how to talk to other humans, a strangeness that I inhabited first with trepidation and then glee. Free from the bondage of another's gaze, my own loosened. I felt *the doing* as I had not since those days in the woods as a child. I shook loose the context of my life and explored it anew. I tasted the pine needles and ate watermelon by the fistful. I reopened the channel inside myself, old enough now to know I was not alone, nor mad, but capable even of finding words for its fiery power.

Most of all, I experienced a radical change in my relationship to my own body. That instinct for self-love that I had glimpsed at twelve and worked so hard to exile had been waiting for me all those years. I bought a new bed, and every morning I woke alone and gently patted myself down, as if taking inventory of my valuable cargo. Good morning, hips. Good morning, thighs. Good morning, hands. I stared at them with that old sense of wonder. It was just us, for three whole months, and then the better part of a year. Eating whatever I hungered for. The late-night reading and list writing. The silvery wordless mornings.

How wrong I had been about freedom. I had mistakenly thought that beauty was the price of it, that I must succeed at erasing myself in order to be myself. In fact, it was the opposite. Only when I divested from the systems that benefited from my self-hatred could I relinquish it and glimpse freedom. As Lorde promised, "when we begin to live from within outward, in touch with the power of the erotic within ourselves . . . then we begin to be responsible for ourselves in the deepest sense."

I had only wanted to change my way of loving and being loved. I didn't know that doing so would return me to myself. If the erotic is "a measure between the beginnings of our sense of self and the chaos of our strongest feelings," my hands are, and have always been, erotic instruments. They were the first conduits, the first actors of that chaos of strongest feelings, inextricably bound to my sense of self as a child. After years of estrangement, they pointed the way back.

That year I began assigning my creative writing students the task of writing a love letter to the part of their body with which they have the most fraught relationship. It has ever since been a regular part of my curriculum. The students find it extremely difficult. However painful, we often cherish our own self-hatreds, mistake them as intrinsic to our survival. After they write these letters, however, after they read them with tremorous voices and flushed faces, there is wildness in their eyes, as if a door has opened, as if a tiny flame has lit deep inside them. I would cup my hands around each one if I could.

Six months into our relationship, a year after my celibacy ended, Donika and I spent a long sunny Saturday wandering around Toronto, holding hands.

"Will you tell me something that you like about me?" I asked as the sun heavied with afternoon, made everything slow and golden.

"Of course," she said. "What kind of thing?"

"Hmm," I said. "A shallow thing?" It was the sort of exchange that had already become a convention of our relationship. In the very beginning, we had agreed to ask for exactly what we wanted from each other and had both kept that promise. How simple it was, and how long it had taken. It had required all of my previous relationships, a decade of therapy, and nearly a year of celibacy to learn how to identify what I needed, how to ask for it, and finally, how to receive it. In this and so many other ways our love felt like the culmination of so many years' work.

"Something that I like about you"—she smiled—"is that you are not very tall."

I laughed. Moments before, I had commented on how comfortable I was in the sneakers I'd worn for our day of walking. It was rare for me to wear sneakers for anything but jogging. I had worn heels of some kind almost every day since my late teens.

"But if I were taller, I could wear shoes like that," I said, stopping at a boutique window to point at a sleek pair of oxfords.

"Why can't you wear them now?" she asked, genuinely baffled.

I grimaced. "My legs are so short and my hands and feet are so big. I'd look like a little troll," I explained. I'd never been this honest with a lover about my preoccupation with disguising my true form, my belief that it needed a disguise. I might have learned what freedom was, but my ability to live it was still limited in these small and tenacious ways.

Like my past lovers, Donika is taller than me and dresses mostly in clothes designed for men. The similarities end there.

I don't mean that her hands are bigger than mine, though they are. I mean that the roles we assume in our relationship don't fall into gendered categories, in or out of the bedroom. It's part of what makes it possible for me to share with her these inhibitions; I am certain that she doesn't need me to play the girl. We just get to be ourselves.

"Do you know what else has a small body and big hands and feet?" she asked me.

I shook my head.

"A baby tiger," she said. "They are very strong and nimble. They are excellent swimmers and climbers, in addition to being extremely cute."

As I laughed, she turned her body to face mine. When she spoke, her voice was gentle but firm. "Little friend," she said, "I am charmed by your proportions. Just because you have an issue with them doesn't mean that anyone else does." She looked back at the window. "I think you'd look great in those shoes."

Part of learning to receive things is learning to do so when you haven't even asked for them. To let love sneak up on you with its warm splash of light and just stand there squinting. It can be a lot to take. I stood there for a minute, not sure if I was going to cry. I didn't. We kept walking.

In canto 6 of his epic satire *Don Juan,* Byron contemplates his own adoration of all women, and muses about the Hecatoncheire, "enviable Briareus . . . with thy hands and heads . . . hads't all things multiplied in proportion." To which I say: only a man would think one hundred dicks better than one. Only a person who doesn't know that *thy hands and heads* can indeed *be* all things.

Today, my love has no aversion to being fucked. Our fucking is no partially clothed, one-way activity. When my long fingers, my strong fingers, slide inside her, she writhes and mews and grunts. Yes, like an animal. We are animals, never more than now.

For a sliver of time, I sometimes step out of myself, like a wheel that's lost its track. I see my body crouched over her, thighs flexed, back slick with sweat, face dumb with desire, mouth open—and I shudder, ready to tuck it all back in and make myself small again. To do that would mean leaving her here alone in this bed, leaving this *here* that exists only between both of our bodies. So, I don't. I blink twice and step back into myself.

More, she instructs me, and I have more to give her. My hands are enormous. They are brazenly big, unabashedly big, hungry and huge and beloved. The desire they enact, this desire we share, is earthquakes and sea storms. It blinds our thoughts and clenches our eyes and makes us pray to gods we don't believe in. It washes us onto the shore of the bed, slack and salt-crusted, wrecked by pleasure. All that time, I thought it was my hands who needed to shrink, when it was I who needed to grow into them.

Once, after fucking me, she said, "There is a word in my mind, but I don't know if I can say it. It's going to sound silly."

"Tell me," I said, my head on her chest, mouth briny with her.

"Sublime. Fucking you feels like the sublime."

I laughed and rolled onto my back, threw my arm over my eyes.

"It is!" she insisted. "Sometimes it scares me. I feel like I could just lose myself in it."

"We call that sublime," Kant wrote, "which is absolutely great" and marked by "beyond all comparison." A thing that can inspire us to feel a fearfulness, "without being afraid *of* it." An earthquake, for example, Kant understood as a sublime event.

I knew exactly what Donika meant, but I had no words to name it. My knowing was from a time before I knew such experience was speakable. Our sex does not feel like an exchange of power, but like a natural event that can only occur when both of us stop thinking of ourselves and trust our bodies completely. No one plays the boy, because no one *plays* anything. It can't happen unless we trust that we'll be loved at our most animal.

Intimacy, I've found, has little to do with romance. Maybe it is the opposite of romance, which is based on a story written by someone else. It is a closeness to another person that requires closeness with oneself. It is not watching lightning strike from the window but being struck by it.

True love is not the reward for a successful campaign to domesticate oneself. It is the thing I was practicing all of those years ago, in my own constructive play. It is entering the woods a stranger, shaking loose the stories assigned you, and naming the world as you meet it, together.

It is true that I am loved now for exactly the things I have tried to erase in myself, but this isn't a story about love teaching me to love myself. It's not even about the decision to love myself. Loving myself has never been something I was able to do simply by deciding to.

This is a love story, though. The kind where the lover laments all the years she lost at the altar of some false god. When regret seeps in, I try to remember the Hecatoncheires. They did not defeat the Titans as children. They lived under their power. They were *of* the Titans. It took years for their strength to surpass that of the old gods. But when they did? They threw mountains, a hundred at a time, one for each great hand. And what if they had been taught to hate their own strength? Maybe it would have taken a hundred years for them to grasp a mountain in hand, to understand what they could do, that they could make their own Olympus.

I did not
choose to be
a spectacle.

INTRUSIONS

In the summer of 2004, when Montrose Avenue was still Bushwick, and George W. Bush was the incumbent president, my best friend and I moved into a duplex on the same block as the L train with her two pit bulls. It was the nicest apartment I'd ever lived in, cheaply refurbished with parquet floors and shiny fixtures that went wobbly within our first month. My friend took the basement and my bedroom was on the building's ground floor, with two big street-facing windows. Every few minutes the train rumbled underneath us, but despite the stream of commuters that rushed by my windows all day, I kept my curtains open, reveling in the abundance of natural light.

I was near the end of my four-year tenure as a pro-domme. I was also newly sober. All of which to say that I spent a lot of time at home reading novels and self-help books instead of drinking and shooting heroin.

One night, after I'd turned off my reading light but not yet sunk into sleep, an uneasy feeling swept up my back. John Cheever, in his story "The Cure," which tells of a suburban man being peeped on by his male neighbor, aptly describes the physical response to being watched as a "terrible hardening of the flesh." I was accustomed to the sweep of shadows along the walls as the train emptied its passengers and they marched next to my windows, and cars braked at the corner stoplight, but one shadow had stopped, its source blocking the stripe of light at the corner of my closest window.

"Hey, baby," a voice murmured from outside. "Are you sleeping?"

My face went cold and my body stiffened. My heart battered inside my chest.

"Pretty girl," said the voice. "You touching yourself?"

The voice was so close, just a couple yards away from my bed. I wanted to scream, to flee the room, but was too terrified of indicating my presence to move. Instead, I started to pray—whether to God or the interloper, I didn't know. *Please stop*, I pleaded silently. *Please let this not be happening. Please go away.* After a few more murmurings, he did. The light reappeared at the crack of my curtains and his shadow slid along the length of the windows, a twin darkness slipping across the wall inside my bedroom.

My pulse thrummed and I remained still for a long time after that, petrified that he would return, but he didn't. Not that night. When my mind settled enough to think, I realized that he couldn't possibly have seen me. The curtains covered the windows, and anyway, peering into my dark bedroom from the streetlight-bathed sidewalk, he would only have seen his own reflection in the glass.

How could he have known that I was even a woman? It seemed wildly unlikely that he would have gambled on any random inhabitant. I might have been a bodybuilder or an off-duty cop, watching *Unsolved Mysteries* or the UFC semifinals, tossing raw meat to my monstrous dog. No, I realized, he hadn't seen me then. He had seen me before. I frantically scrolled through days past to remember if I had noticed anyone lurking, noticed anyone specific outside my windows at all. I hadn't. Then I skimmed my daytime bedroom activities, imagined the night prowler secretly observing me staring at my computer, reading in bed, carelessly returning from a shower without remembering to close the curtains for a few naked moments as I stared into my closet or the mirror.

This revelation that my privacy had been an illusion made me feel skinless. He could have been stalking me for weeks or months before mustering the nerve or will to speak. That unknown span of time seethed behind me, a room filling with smoke.

I grew up in the woods of New England, where we didn't even have curtains on our bedroom windows, as there was no light pollution, no passersby, and hardly a neighbor within yelling distance. When I moved to New York City, I was shocked by the relentless verbal appraisal of men in public spaces. "Street harassment" wasn't a common phrase in 1999, but the experience was as common as rats on the subway tracks. By 2004 I was used to it, deft at discerning the likelihood of a catcaller's retaliation if I ignored him, instinctively knowing whether to smile demurely or stonewall. In all cases, a woman had to keep it moving and could never argue without threat of physical violence. The constant vigilance required outdoors rendered domestic spaces holy in their privacy. Every woman in New York, and perhaps any city, knows her bodily relief after the apartment door is shut and locked behind her. The violation of that sanctity filled me with panic.

Why me? I wondered. Had I unknowingly done something to court the midnight lurker? Was it possible that I *had* masturbated while he was watching some afternoon past? In hindsight, the innocence of my former self seemed irresponsible. Culpable, even. How naive, how brazenly uncareful, I had been to stand naked in my own bedroom. I had never heard of such a thing happening to anyone I knew. Of course,

I had never asked if such things had happened to anyone I knew, and it is counterinstinctual to volunteer these stories. The belief in our own culpability encourages our silence, and our silence protects the lie of our culpability.

As a precociously developed eleven-year-old, I never told anyone about Alex, who spat on me every day at the bus stop. At twelve, I never told anyone about the grown man who groped me in a friend's bathroom. At thirteen, I never spoke a word of the sexual harassment I withstood for a year of junior high school. At fourteen, I never told anyone about the sixty-year-old manager of the tackle shop that employed me and his endless stream of dirty jokes. At nineteen, I never told anyone about the man who jerked off onto my back while I was asleep after I refused to have sex with him.

No doubt, my internalization of our victim-blaming culture is largely to blame for this silence. Of course the man outside my window hadn't seen me masturbating, but while we have no familiar narrative for why men do such things, we all know the ways women invite their victimization by walking after dark, wearing short skirts, or having big breasts. The pathology of victimhood would also claim that self-blaming and shame were my very ordinary attempt to explain what had happened to me, to assert control over it by assuming responsibility.

But also, consider *Body Double*. In Brian De Palma's homage to Hitchcock's *Rear Window* and *Vertigo*, a woman dances provocatively before her window every night dressed in only lacy panties and a belly chain (proof of the film's 1984 release date). The performance ends with a stagy roll around on the bed that gestures toward masturbation but is pure performance for the male viewer.

Had I seen *Body Double*? I don't remember, and it doesn't matter—this narrative, of the woman self-consciously performing for an invisible male audience, has saturated our culture. I'm not saying that it's never sexy to be watched. Exhibitionism is as real as voyeurism. One of the many friends and acquaintances I interviewed about being peeped on claimed of her reclusive neighbor: "I allow him to, as it's probably the most exciting part of his life. I pretend not to see him until the very end, when I turn the shower off. Then I just look at him briefly. It's kind of hot."

There is an everydayness to the eroticism of her story, partly because we've all been indoctrinated by the onslaught of messaging that this is hot, partly because it's hot to be wanted. "Didn't you like the attention?" asked the boyfriend of a woman I interviewed after she told him about her peeper.

It is also a narrative that exonerates men. The more plausible it seems that women are always performing, the less indictable the watching. If we want it, where is the crime?

Better yet, make us seductresses, inverting men's role even more extremely: they are *our* victims! In the fourth episode of David Fincher's popular Netflix series *Mindhunter*, after two FBI agents interview the rapist and serial killer of five women, Monte Rissell, one of them, observes: "So Rissell's the real victim here?" His partner responds, "That's how he sees it." One of the most shared qualities of all predators is their self-conception of victimhood.

The term "peeping Tom" originates from Lady Godiva's alleged eleventh-century ride through Coventry nude on horseback, an event still commemorated by Coventry citizens every year by a (clothed) march through the city. Supposedly the townspeople swore to avert their eyes, and all made good on the promise except for one "peeping Tom." It is no cautionary tale. After all, who could blame the original Tom for not enjoying the spectacle freely offered?

We are bombarded not just with suggestions that women are always performing for men but also with prescriptions for doing so, from the moment we are able to take direction. "A man's presence," John Berger writes in *Ways of Seeing*, "is dependent on the promise of power he embodies . . . A man's presence suggests what he is capable of doing to you or for you." Conversely, "how a woman appears to a man can determine how she is treated. To acquire some control over this process, women must contain it and interiorize it."

By my early twenties, I had already undergone a long education in this. I had suffered the consequences of all the ways I could not or did not control how I appeared to men. I had implanted that gaze inside myself. I had tried to suppress my animal nature, to change the shape of my body, to erase myself in a hundred ways, to give men exactly what they wanted, and none of it had worked. I understood how easy it was for men to justify doing anything they wanted to a woman. I had learned about the male gaze in women's studies classes, but knew no way to dig it out of me.

My own continued attention to the gazes of men felt incriminating. Wasn't it my job to be desired by them? I had even found a way to get paid for it. In Berger's words, "Men look at women. Women watch themselves being looked at . . . Thus she turns herself into an object—and most particularly an object of vision: a sight." Like Lady Godiva, I had turned myself into a sight, I thought. Of course the stranger had looked.

It is through the collaboration of all these factors, of course, that patriarchy is enforced: an elegant machinery whose pistons fire silently inside our own minds, and whose gleaming gears we mistake for our own jewelry.

The day after that first (known) visit, I taped the curtains to the window frame so there was not even a sliver through which to look. That night I brought Red, the bigger of my roommate's dogs, to bed with me. I lay under the covers, his heavy body curled against my legs as he gently snored. Cars hissed by, the curtains glowing with their passing headlights. I was wide awake when he came.

"Hey baby," he said, his form darkening the window. "Are you ready for me?" My body tingled with adrenaline, and I squeezed Red's paw with one hand. "Is that pussy wet for me?" the voice asked. Red's ears jumped, from the sound, my touch, or the scent of my fear. He was more interested in snuggling and treats than guarding against intruders, but he was easily disturbed by noises outside and made an imposing figure at seventy pounds of pure muscle. He raised himself up and gave a hearty bark.

The wave of relief I felt simply at having another presence validate the disturbance was so great that I took a heaving breath. Red stood on the bed now, ears trembling, and emitted a low whine. My relief created a tiny breach in the fear, and through it rushed a geyser of fury. Under a lifetime of vigilance and fear of bodily harm often lies a bedrock of rage. Who was this asshole? I was suddenly irate at the thought of having been paralyzed with fear in my own bed.

I pushed back the covers and sat up, my bare feet thudding the floor. Red followed me out of my bedroom, where I slipped into a coat and sneakers and clipped a leash onto his collar. I exited the apartment and the building's front door. I must have assumed that the culprit would have fled at the barking, because I was surprised to find him still standing outside my window. A man in his twenties, brown hair, black puffer jacket. He casually loped toward me.

"What the fuck are you doing?" I asked, holding Red's leash close to give the impression that he was bloodthirsty when actually I wanted to prevent him from lunging forward to lick the stranger's hands in friendly greeting.

"Hey girl," he said, looking me up and down. "How's your night going? You busy?"

"Are you kidding me?" I asked.

"You have a boyfriend?" he asked.

"You need to get the fuck out of here and never come back," I said. "I'll be calling the cops." Before he could answer, I spun around and dragged Red back into the building. My pulse pounding in my ears, I wondered if it had been a mistake to let him see my face.

He didn't come back that night, but I still couldn't sleep. His reaction had confused me. There had been no evidence of shame on his face, no acknowledgment that he had done anything inappropriate, let alone threatening. There hadn't been any particular menace in his manner as he propositioned me. He'd acted just like so many men I passed in the street every day: as though I were a legitimate sexual interest, a woman drinking at the same bar instead of someone he'd been harassing and stalking. As though these behaviors all fell under the same umbrella of romantic pursuit.

In *Body Double*, our protagonist peeps on his neighbor, stalks her for an entire day, watches her in a lingerie-store dressing room, eavesdrops at a pay phone on her conversation, and recovers a pair of her newly purchased panties from a trash can. When she finally confronts him, barely a few words shared between them, she falls into his arms and they start madly kissing. Not only is she is attracted to him despite his stalking, but it is offered as the only evidence of seduction. That this makes any narrative sense is owed to the entire first third of the movie being devoted to humanizing the hero. In the opening scene, he returns home to find his girlfriend in bed with another man, and we go on to witness his tearful recall of childhood bullying, his episodes of crippling claustrophobia, and his trials as a struggling actor.

Had my stalker seen *Body Double*? Who knows. He had plenty other opportunities to observe this narrative. The 1983 hit movie *Revenge of the Nerds*, for instance, in which a group of lovable college outcasts plant a camera in the showers of the women's dormitory and sell nude photos of one of its inhabitants. After one of the nerds tricks the woman into having sex with him while disguised as another man, she unveils his true identity and admits that she is in love with him. That is: peeping, humiliation, and rape constitute the courtship of their romance.

There is also *Malicious, Animal House, Stripes, Porky's, Once Upon a Time in America, American Beauty, The Girl Next Door, You Will Meet a Tall Dark Stranger,* and *Stranger Things.* I could go on and on and on.

Just as these productions encourage men to believe that stalking and peeping are acceptable forms of courtship, likely to resolve in a love match, so do they prescribe to women a desire to be the object of such behavior. I did wonder, as I lay in bed fully clothed after our confrontation: Had I somehow misread the experience and overreacted? I knew that I hadn't.

A few years previous, I might have been more able to perform the mental acrobatics necessary to discredit my own instincts, to exile the feeling of profound violation. Maybe that inability is partially owed to the narrative as familiar as that of the benevolent love interest peeper: the voyeuristic killer. So prevalent is this depiction that, again, a full catalog isn't needed. A few years ago I instituted a personal ban on television shows that featured the violent assaults of women as central plot points. They are too many to count, and they saturate the spectrum from lowbrow tabloid crime dramas to award-winning paid cable network shows directed by and starring Hollywood royalty: *Prime Suspect, The Fall, The Killing, True Detective, Mindhunter,* and *Law & Order: Special Victims Unit,* the second-longest-running scripted prime-time television show in history. To think of the millions of Americans absorbing these images of peeped and stalked and subsequently mutilated women's bodies chills me. They keep making them because we keep watching them. I didn't stop watching for political reasons, though. It wasn't a boycott. I stopped watching because I couldn't bear to collect any more of those images in my imagination, especially as a woman living alone in New York City.

A big difference between the two cultural narratives about peeping—that of the harmless romantic lead and that of the violent—is that one is much truer than the other. *Homicide Studies* reports that 89 percent of murdered women were also stalked within twelve months of their killing, and 54 percent of murdered women reported stalking to the police before-hand. Carmen, one of my interviewees, reported spotting a peeper outside her window just a few nights before an intruder broke into her apartment and raped her roommate. He was never caught, though a series of similar crimes were reported a year or so later. Another woman was reluctant to call the police on her peeping neighbor and later read of his suicide just before a third conviction of pedophilia.

Many of those television narratives boast of being pulled from real headlines, a fact that obscures the reality that nearly half of all murders of women are not done by sociopathic strangers but by romantic partners. The headlines about such murders often include phrases like "Romeo and Juliet Style Attack" and "Murdered for Love."

This is why the narratives in which the line between danger and romance gets purposefully blurred are most troubling to me. In *Body Double*, a *different* stalker is offered as the dangerous one, rendering our hero even more benign in relief. While our protagonist is stalking his neighbor, so is a grotesque giant—"The Indian"—who ends up gruesomely murdering the woman with an electric drill and is later revealed to be a different handsome white man in disguise. Peeping, *Body Double* insists, is as likely to be a precursor to romance as it is to murder. When we are supposed to yield to our stalkers and when to run from them is left up to us. It is a compelling plot device and a timeworn method of gaslighting women out of trusting their instincts; De Palma far from invented it.

Body Double is a tribute to Hitchcock's *Vertigo* (1958), and borrows generously from its plot, in which Scottie, a private eye played by James Stewart who suffers from extreme vertigo, is hired to tail Kim Novak's Madeline. As in *Body Double*, our heroine falls in love with the man on seemingly no basis beyond his stalking her. There is another bad man covertly orchestrating his own macabre plot, and Madeline is also murdered at the film's conclusion. De Palma's other inspiration for *Body Double*, Hitchcock's *Rear Window*, similarly features James Stewart as a heroic peeper who spies on his comely dancing neighbor and eventually reveals another neighbor who has murdered his own wife.

My mother loved *Rear Window* as a girl, and my whole family watched it during my childhood, laughing together in surprise at every plot twist. *Vertigo* was also a favorite of mine as a younger woman—I spent a few months in pencil skirts, trying to wrestle my hair into a French twist as sleek as Kim Novak's. Revisiting all of these films, however, left me glancing over my shoulder every time I left the apartment, torn between wanting to stay home and to punch every man who walked too close behind me.

The only famous peeping film I hadn't seen before writing this was *Peeping Tom*. Widely hailed as a masterpiece, it is distinct for its abandonment of the dichotomy between the benevolent stalker and the murderous one; its subject embodies both. The handsome blond Mark is a serial killer who videotapes the terrified faces of his female victims at the moment of death and compulsively rewatches them. When his guileless downstairs neighbor Helen (who he meets by peering into her window) attempts to draw him out, he reveals to her that his father was a famous psychologist who performed experiments on his son like putting lizards on his bed and filming the boy's terrified responses. Helen volleys between falling in love with Mark, sympathizing with his trauma, and fearing for her own safety. It is a comprehensive illustration of what women are expected to be for the man in their lives: the person he exerts power over, the one who listens to and sympathizes with him, the object on which to project his romantic fantasies of purity and exceptionalism, and his savior.

"Sure," a friend quipped about the film, "being a woman and getting murdered sucks, but it's not as bad as having a MEAN DADDY."

It shouldn't come as any great surprise, I guess, to find that the creators of narratives that humanize dangerous men and confuse fear with seduction often have a personal investment in this depiction. Tippi Hedren, the star of Hitchcock's *The Birds* and *Marnie*, explains in her 2016 memoir that the auteur sexually assaulted her more than once and retaliated after she rejected him by tormenting her on set. Hitchcock allegedly insisted that other cast members ostracize Hedren, subjected her to the pecking of live birds for five days of filming, and then blackballed her career, which never recovered.

Woody Allen, who features peeping in *Radio Days* and *You Will Meet a Tall Dark Stranger*, has gone unpunished for his crimes, though they are well known by now, as are those of the fugitive rapist Roman Polanski, in whose films peeping and stalking are a hallmark.

While gathering sources for this essay, I immediately thought of James Ellroy, the celebrated crime writer of *The Black Dahlia*, *L.A. Confidential*, and *My Dark Places*, who has featured peeping Toms in many of his novels. A cursory search led me to a 2013 video interview with Walter Kirn, in which Ellroy describes his own history of peeping on women in Los Angeles in the late 1960s, and breaking into their homes by way of their pet doors to steal their underwear. Upon first watch, I was aghast, and rewound the video to watch it again.

"Here's the thing about this, Walter," says Ellroy about halfway through, clearly enjoying himself. "I broke into houses, in the manner I just described, seventeen, eighteen, twenty, twenty-one, twenty-three times, tops. From late '66 to the summer of '69." Ellroy doesn't just describe the events; he brags about them. After recounting one such "great night," he slowly intones, "Missy M's bra . . . It's indelible." He tells Kirn, "You take it home with you, brother."

"You could've put these skills to actual use," Kirn muses in response. "'Cause you're describing a reporter to me!" Kirn may have been horrified. His smile as Ellroy speaks looks unnatural. Instead of objecting, however, he plays the amiable interviewer and characterizes the predatory behavior as journalistic. By accepting the other man's invitation to bond over the violation of those women, he reinforces the long tradition of men bonding over the dehumanization of women.

Revenge of the Nerds, after all, isn't a movie about men seducing women by humiliating and assaulting them; that is just a plot device to support the real story, about the bonding of a group of underdogs against a group of more powerful men.

The Cheever story is also solely interested in women as a backdrop for his tableau of masculinity, though in this case featuring conflict rather than collaboration. When the narrator of "The Cure" spots his peeping neighbor on the train platform, the apparent purity of the man's daughter persuades our narrator not to confront the peeper. Instead, seemingly as consolation, the narrator follows a different young woman off of the train. "She looked at me once," he tells the reader, "and she knew that I was following her, but I felt sure she was the kind of woman who would not readily call for help." He goes on to explain, "It was all I could do to keep from saying to her, very, very softly, 'Madame, will you please let me put my hand around your ankle? That's all I want to do, madame. It will save my life.'" We are meant to be impressed by how deeply the protagonist is affected by the neighbor's violation, and by his impending divorce. His behavior is weird, but not unsympathetic. Bachelorhood and the intrusion on his privacy seem to have agitated a deep well of aggression whose contents require some receptacle or outlet. He's not a creep; he is reclaiming his masculine presence, so "dependent on the promise of power he embodies," and passing on the baton of victimhood. The woman's fear assures him that he is no longer the object, but the subject.

Though I threatened it, I didn't seriously consider calling the police. My instinct was to blame myself, and I assumed that they would too. They would say that I was overreacting, and on some level, I hoped that I was. I didn't share the entitlement of the narrator of "The Cure," who says, "The situation, on the surface, was ridiculous, and I could see that, but the dread of seeing his face in the window again was real and cumulative, and I didn't see why I should have to endure it, particularly at a time when I was trying to overhaul my whole way of living." His belief in his right to pursue his better life undisturbed allows him to call the local police, though when he does, the cop claims the force is too small to send a guard to his house. Masculinity, as we know, is no cakewalk, but at least he is permitted to address his trauma by paying it forward almost immediately afterward in the disempowerment of the woman on the train.

That dynamic corroborates much of the research on the pathology of voyeurs, which claims that they, like so many predators, are paying the power trip forward. A 2016 article in the journal *Sexual Addiction & Compulsivity* tells us that a large percentage of paraphiliacs report early sexual abuse and, especially in the case of voyeurs, a slew of other social and psychiatric burdens that include negative relationships with their fathers.

Still, we don't need to trace these behaviors back to early trauma to explain them, because the male ego doesn't need to suffer a wound so grave as that of childhood abuse to enact this response. Rejection is sometimes enough. One can simply look at the men in New York City's streets, who will often respond venomously to being simply ignored, or to Brent Ball, a classmate of mine in high school.

Brent was a legend in tenth grade. A year behind him, I had heard all of the stories. Girls who had sworn to wait until marriage lost their minds when he entered a room, and later, their virginities. He was a heartbreaker, but he didn't break my heart, not in the rumored way. At a party one night he cornered me, and after some cursory making out, tried to solicit a blow job. I refused, wrongly assuming our intimacy would end with that brief physical transaction. We didn't speak again for a year.

A few months after that incident, I became involved with my first girlfriend, Lillian. I was madly in love for the first time and spent weekends biking across town to her home, which was nestled amid cranberry bogs—dry moors in the off season, but crimson when the berries bloomed, before they were flooded. One afternoon, on a long walk, we stopped to kiss on a path beside one of these bogs. Kissing became groping, and for a few minutes we rolled around in the dried leaves, tugging at each other's clothing to expose precious patches of bare skin. We were normally somewhat chaste, and so that tousle by the bog was, for about eighteen hours, one of my sweetest and most exhilarating memories.

The next morning in school, I passed Brent in the hallway, a not uncommon occurrence. To my surprise, he paused to speak.

"Hey, Melissa," he said with a smirk. "I saw you yesterday."

"What?" I said, baffled. "Where?"

"On the bog, with your friend." He stared at me for a moment longer, to watch it sink in, and then sauntered away. My face hot, I scrolled back through time, just as I would a decade later, after my talking Tom's first visit. Had he been following us? Had he followed me other times? Where had he been hiding? The unknowable details clouded the whole day previous, and possible other days. I pictured him crouched in the woods, leering at us, and my own past ignorance, the searing vulnerability of it. There was no way then to name that violation, and no one to name it to. So I just swallowed it. Like so many other things, I suspected that I had brought it upon myself.

My stalker returned to the window, sometimes two or three times per week. Each time, I clutched the barking Red and stared at the knife I'd begun keeping beside the bed, but I didn't go outside again. I had already forgotten his face and worried during the days that I might pass him in the street and be recognized. As one of the women I interviewed said after expressing similar fear, "it could have been anyone."

There were other reasons that I didn't want to go to the police. At the time, I was still a sex worker, which further complicated things, both externally and internally. I wasn't interested in the police discovering what I did for a living. It was also literally my job at that time to perform the erotic fantasies of men. As Berger said, I had made myself an object, a sight. It was impossible for me not to internalize the idea that my purpose was to perform erotically for men, even if the form that performance usually took was of their own humiliation. The difference between what happened at work and when my stalker came at night *felt* clear inside me—labor versus terror—but while I understood the concept of consent when it came to my clients and the world of S&M, it didn't occur to me in those terms when that man spoke into my window. In 2017, Alana Massey wrote an editorial in *Self* that asserts, "Sex workers do not exist to save abusive men from themselves, or to save non-sex-working women from abusive men. Every sex worker ought to have the ability to establish her own boundaries, her own rates, and not face intimidation when she does not give consent for any reason." But at twenty-three, I hadn't read anything like that.

I was also deeply invested in a nonjudgmental view of kinks and fetishes, among which voyeurism is ordinary. Paraphiliacs were my bread and butter, and my friends. Even now, writing this, I am reluctant to publicize the pathological contexts. I know now, as I did then, that kink can be healthy, that its practitioners are often highly processed persons capable of profound intimacy. I'm well aware of how the pathologization of "atypical" sexual practices has been used to punish, oppress, criminalize, and stigmatize people like me and my former clients for centuries. Because those practices have been marginalized for so long, there still isn't a familiar enough public discourse on them for the layperson to differentiate between the healthy and the harmful. I worry that the casual reader will conflate them, as our culture has been so long doing. The difference between consensual voyeuristic practices and nonconsensual is analogous to that between sex and rape. By condemning these practices wholesale, we make it that much easier to erase their complexity, the vast spectrum on which they function.

As a domme, my voyeuristic clients seemed especially harmless. The men who came into the dungeon with fantasies of peeping seemed a far cry from the ones who wanted us to crush bugs with our bare feet, tell stories of cannibalism, or shit on them. Whatever my personal feeling about their fetishes, none of these people were abusive. The difference between my clients, who had our consent to play out these fantasies, and those who practice voyeurism without their victims' consent is not only critical but criminal. Still, the authors of "Varieties of Intrusion: Exhibitionism and Voyeurism" write: "Historically, exhibitionism and voyeurism were often viewed as nuisance crimes which had little impact on the victim and occurred in isolation." This impression is likely due to the representations in popular culture, but also because the impulse to peep isn't so strange.

I like to look in people's windows, too. As the subway trundles home, I peer into the yellow-lit windows of strangers' apartments, coveting those glimpses into their dioramic lives. Passing through wealthier neighborhoods, who doesn't like to spy through the windows of brownstones and ogle the glamorous chandeliers and custom bookshelves? Most of us are curious about each other, enjoy imagining the alternate lives we might be living, the rooms we might inhabit. Also, it can be titillating. A 2006 study found that 83 percent of men and 74 percent of women claimed that they would watch someone undressing if they would not be caught.

How do we reconcile that number with the 1987 study that found 37 percent of voyeurs involved in rape and 52 percent in pedophilia? Or another, which concluded that a quarter of all serial victim murderers are voyeurs? We don't have to. "Varieties of Intrusion: Exhibitionism and Voyeurism" claims that "the roots of these behaviors are integrated into the normative sexual template; however, individuals engaging in exhibitionism and voyeurism display these normative behaviors in pathological or addictive patterns, rather than in the course of adaptive relationship development." The argument has long been made that all our harmful actions progress out of a perversion of "natural" instincts, and that the prosecution of thought crimes would find all of us guilty. Despite our acknowledged impulses, however, only a small percentage of the general population has been found to practice voyeurism. A minority of those who practice voyeurism progress to other behaviors, though my peeper was one of those.

"I was sitting by the window of my Portland apartment one night," explained Hallie. "And this man slid a ripped-out page from a porn magazine through the cracked window. It was a woman giving a blow job." She laughed. "As if I was going to be like, 'Oh, that looks really fun.'" When I asked her how she responded, she said, "I just waved a gun around, like, 'Hey baby, where are you?' and heard this mad crashing in the bushes outside as he ran away." Hallie was an outlier among my interviews, most of whom didn't have a boyfriend at the time who was "the type to keep a lot of guns around."

Jill, for instance, was working as a stripper and had just moved out of an apartment she shared with an abusive boyfriend. "I felt free and safe," she said of living alone. Until a note appeared on her front door that read: "My friends and I love watching you work out. We have been watching you for over a week now. We particularly like it when you bend over and we can see your pussy in your underwear from behind.

We talk about how we're going to fuck you from behind. We will make you cum and feel really good." Terrified and furious, she resolved to get blackout shades, but that same night she found another note, this time taped to her bedroom window: "We are looking into your bedroom window. We can't wait to bend you every way over the bed. We are going to fuck you till you bleed and scream. I hope you don't mind, we find you very sexy. Signed, your secret admirers."

"What the ever-loving fuck?" she commented. "'We hope you don't mind'? That was the scariest part. The nice handwriting, the good grammar, the faux-gentlemanly interest in my feelings and pleasure." She called friends to come stay over that night, but still couldn't sleep. Three days later there was a third letter: "We hope you have considered our offer. You are very sexy. We look forward to fucking you in all three holes while you scream and cry. Signed, your secret admirers." She didn't trust the police, but still called them. "That's how scared I was."

"What do you want us to do?" the police officer asked.

"What can you do?"

"We can drive by your house a couple of times. But we can't sit outside and watch."

"Do you think this will get worse? Do you think they'll actually do something?" she asked.

"My guess is that they will."

"What would you do if you were me?"

"Lady . . ." The cop sighed. "I hate to tell you this, but if I were you, I would move."

So she did.

Jill's story horrified me more than most, because it was the closest to my own. I suspected that the voyeur who graduated to dirty talk might be the kind who would progress to other actions. Despite my reservations, I walked the half mile to the nearest police station.

I wore a collared shirt with long sleeves to cover my tattoos, which quickly dampened with sweat in the summer heat. The counter rose almost to my chin, and I peered over it on tiptoes as I shivered in the chilly air-conditioned precinct. I explained my situation to an officer who listened with a patience that seemed overperformed. When I finished speaking, he squinted at me.

"Now, do you know this man?"

"No," I said. "I told you, I only saw him the one time, when I confronted him. I'd never seen him before."

He grimaced slightly. "You're sure? You never went out with him? This isn't some boyfriend of yours?"

I was shocked, though I shouldn't have been.

"What I want to know is what you can do about it," I said after a pause.

"Well, since you don't know him, you can't file a restraining order."

"Can you send someone to watch for him?"

The cop didn't laugh, but almost. "The best thing you can do is call when he's there, and we can send someone over."

I wrote down the number to call with shaking hands, knowing how unlikely it was. The last thing I wanted to do was speak when he was outside the window. Though in general I was loathe to call the police, I had done it years before when a man was attempting to rape a woman outside my previous apartment. I had been amazed by how long they took to arrive. They ended up finding him, that time, a man convicted of previous rapes, and I had served as a witness in a hearing.

One of the most common denominators in the stories I heard from women was of other men dismissing the peeping, as has long been done to so many forms of abuse. Freud himself considered the incest reports of his female patients to be fantasies. A high school friend of one of my interviews admitted to her years later that he and many of her other male friends used to spy on her getting undressed with binoculars.

"He seemed to think it was a compliment," she told me. Another woman managed to get video footage and the license plate number of her peeper, and still the police did nothing. One woman didn't ever call the police on her peeping mail carrier because she feared being judged for walking naked in her own home. We have all fielded this response to one thing or another. We are exaggerating. We are overreacting. We are villainizing hapless men. Besides, it's flattering. After all, in the hit 1990s sitcom *Married with Children*, when a peeping Tom targets neighborhood women, Peggy Bundy is miffed that she hasn't been victimized and begs her husband, Al, to peep on her.

It is why I cringe when the topic of sexual harassment comes up in the company of men. I fear what they might say, what they might reveal about themselves. Most of them have never experienced it, never even had to think about it before, and their responses reveal the assumptions that line their ignorance.

I thought of this the other night when a friend told me an anecdote over dinner. The school she attends is equipped with an enormous adjacent parking structure—a place, she and I agreed, that all women consider a likely site of assault. My friend happens to be a rape survivor. Like most of the women I know, when returning to her car, she moves speedily with her keys in hand, constantly scanning for potential attackers.

One day a man followed behind her, closer than normal, until she finally spun around and shouted, "Where are you going?" He simply pointed to his nearby car.

When she recounted this experience to her boyfriend—a man everyone remarks upon as a consummate sweetheart—he said, "Well, how do you think it made him feel that you were so afraid of him?"

Not all men! cry the good ones. They don't want to be feared, so it is our job to fix our fear. That is, sure, being a woman who gets assaulted and fears it at every turn sucks, but it's not as bad as getting your feelings hurt. It is the job of women to caretake the feelings of good men, even at the cost of our own safety. We are trained from birth to accommodate them and their uncontrollable urges. Take, for example, the interviewee who caught her onsite landlord peeping on her multiple times. When she went to his wife to complain, the wife simply bought her a pair of blackout curtains.

In 1999 Debra Gwartney's fourteen-year-old daughter saw a man outside her bedroom window, his hand curled around a Panasonic video camera. The police found an upturned bucket taken from their carport and multiple circular rings of indentation in the surrounding dirt where the bucket had been stood upon untold times. (In another interview, a woman found a milk crate outside her window, similar indentations, and a slit in the window screen.)

A year and half later a friend faxed Gwartney a report of William Green's arrest in her town of Eugene, Oregon, when he sent a roll of film to be developed that included an image of an eleven-year-old girl lying on top of him. When the police searched his home, they found dozens of videotapes, going back five years, that included footage of Gwartney's four daughters and more than a hundred others getting dressed and undressed, sleeping, and watching television. A second search found a secret compartment in Green's garage containing more videotapes—including ones of him masturbating in the girls' beds, their panties clutched in his fist—underwear, swimsuits, clots of hair pulled from drains, and photos stolen from Gwartney's family albums.

As I read her account of these horrors, I thought of James Ellroy, celebrated novelist. There is a difference, we say, between victimizing children in this manner and victimizing adults. One of these men acted upon a desire that we abhor and one upon a desire we find more relatable, but they committed many of the same crimes and showed a similar disregard for the rights of their victims.

Just before his trial, Green pleaded guilty as part of a deal. Gwartney's daughters were the only victims to testify at his sentencing hearing. "At the end of the last hearing," Gwartney explained, "the judge said that, really, we were so very lucky that the girls hadn't been touched. This wasn't much of a crime after all: the only things stolen from us were a few pictures, a couple of pairs of underpants. Not one girl's body, he said, had been violated." Though a detective promised Gwartney that Green would never be released from prison, the judge sentenced him only for the burglary charges.

"William Green would not be listed as a sexual predator," said Gwartney. "He would not be denied, upon his release, access to cameras. Schools and neighbors would not be notified of his past behavior. The judge looked down at my daughters from his chair and told them to count themselves fortunate for what had not been done to them. He told my children to leave the courtroom and get on with their lives." Green was released from prison in 2014.

At the conclusion of "The Cure," Cheever's protagonist reunites with his estranged wife. "We've been happy ever since," he writes. As the title suggests, the hero's experience was a foray into his own darkness, a route back to wholesomeness. For a moment, he occupied the violent space of man alone in the world, subject to both the victimization by other men and the violence of his own instincts. In the end, as the final line of the story states, "Everyone here is well."

Not so for the women I interviewed. Their journey was not a foray into their own darknesses, but a subsumption into those of men. "In some ways," Gwartney explains, "the five of us will never get over what happened. We'll not get over the violation of our most private sanctuary by a man who said that as long as he wasn't seen filming girls, he felt he was inflicting harm on no one."

The harm, however, bleeds far into the futures of all the women I interviewed, most of whom struggle to feel at ease in their own homes. "Am I still affected?" asked one woman. "Paranoid is probably the best term for it." Though "paranoid" implies that her vigilance is unwarranted. It points to another lasting effect on many of my interviewees: the worry of their own culpability. "One question burns in me," Gwartney claims, "and I suppose it will keep on burning until the end of my days: When William Green was coming after your children, where the fuck were you?"

Unlike the women I interviewed, I wasn't conscious of how deeply the experience had affected me until recently. Just before I began writing this essay, I told my girlfriend the story of my peeper.

"I never think about it anymore," I explained. "It was terrifying when it happened, but I don't think it stuck with me much after that."

She gave me a quizzical look. "Really? How about the way you keep your curtains closed with double-sided tape?"

"Oh," I said. "I guess I do."

"Or how you won't walk through any windowed room without first putting clothes on, even in the middle of the night?"

"Especially in the middle of the night," I added.

I had never considered how that violation disciplines the way that I inhabit my own home, nearly fifteen years later. How much I had since feared being seen as sexually available to any man passing by. I took for granted that it was always so, because for most of my life, it has been.

This may be the longest effect of a lifetime of being looked at, being told that it is a duty, a compliment, even a source of power: it has eroded my sense of entitlement to privacy. I should never not be thinking of the man who might be watching me, even alone in my bedroom. I should not and cannot refuse a gaze through a window, a neighbor with a camera, a closely following stranger, a comment on the street. How different is a gaze from a hand, after all? What a powerful message it is, that your body ought to be available to any man passing by. It will only inconvenience you to protest. Better to tolerate it. Reframe it as nothing memorable, as a joke, as journalism, as privilege, even as a precursor to love.

My story could have ended any number of ways, and none of them include a romance with my stalker. Like most of the women I interviewed, I moved apartments and rarely thought about this terrifying series of months because it was but one in an endless series of ordinary violations against which I felt impotent to protect myself, except retroactively, in my own words, from many years' distance.

I am lucky that it ended that way, because unlike Lady Godiva, I did not choose to be a spectacle. I cannot make any man promise to look away. Eventually, he stopped coming. But I could never sleep easy after that. I was always listening for some breach in the quiet, some shadow stilled across my bed. Though I moved a few months later and have many times since, I kept waiting.

My darkness
has become
my work
on this earth.

THESMOPHORIA

1. *Kathodos*

Rome, July. The midsummer air thick with cigarette smoke and exhaust. By the time my plane touched down, I'd been awake for almost twenty-four hours, three of which I'd spent waiting at the airport for a rental car. I'd driven into the city amid bleating horns and darting mopeds, parked in a questionable spot, and woven through the crowded sidewalks until I found the address of the tiny apartment I'd rented. Upstairs, I pulled the curtains shut and crawled into the strange bed with its coarse white sheets. I posted a photo on Facebook of my exhausted face—*Italia!*—and instantly fell asleep.

I woke to three text messages from my mother.

You're in Italy??

My ticket is for next month!

Melly???

Months previous, she'd cleared her schedule of psychotherapy patients to meet me in Naples. From there, our plan was to drive to the tiny fishing town on the Sorrento coast where her grandmother had been born, and where I'd rented another apartment for a week. I frantically scrolled through our e-mails, scanning for dates.

It was true. I'd typed the wrong month in our initial correspondence about the trip. Weeks later, we'd forwarded each other our ticket confirmations, which obviously neither of us had closely read.

The panic I felt was more than my disappointment at the ruin of our shared vacation, to which I had so been looking forward. It was more than the sorrow I felt at what must have been her hours of panic while I slept or her imminent disappointment as she corroborated the facts herself. It was more than the fear that she'd be angry with me (who wouldn't be angry with me?), because my mother's anger never lasted.

Imagine a structure as delicate and intricate as honeycomb. One that has weathered many blows, some more careless than others, that could so easily be crushed by the sweeping hand of error. The dread did not rise from my thoughts but from my gut, from some corporeal logic that had kept meticulous track of every mistake before this one. That believed there was a finite number of times one could break someone's heart before it hardened to you.

My mother had wanted a daughter. Melissa, she explained to me, as soon as I was old enough to learn the story, means honeybee. Later I learned that it was the name of the priestesses of Demeter. Melissa, from *meli*, which means honey, like Melindia or Melinoia, those pseudonyms of Persephone. Is it too obvious to compare us to those two?

I don't know how it feels to create a body with my own. Maybe I never will. I remember, though, how my mother nursed me until I was nearly two years old and already speaking in full sentences. When I moved to solid food, she fed me bananas and kefir, whose tartness I still crave. She sang me to sleep against her freckled chest. She read to me and cooked for me and carried me with her everywhere.

What a gift it was to be so loved, to trust in my own safety. All children are built for this, but not all parents rise to the task. Not my birth father, so she left him. We moved in with her mother then. One day on the shore we found him strumming a guitar, the man who became my real father. From the day he and my mother met, he never knew one of us without the other. Now, whenever I see him, one of the first things he always says to me is, "Ah! Just now, you looked exactly like your mother."

They doted on the memory of me as a child, just as they had doted on me when I was a child. Fat and happy, always talking. "You were so cute," they'd say. "We had to watch you. You would have walked off with anyone."

When my father was at sea, it was just my mother and me again. After my brother was born, it was me in whom she confided how much harder it became to say goodbye to my father, year after year. Her tears smelled like sea mist, cool against my cheek. Like they had doted on me, I doted on my brother, our baby.

After my parents separated, they tried nesting—an arrangement where they rotated in and out of the family home while the children remained. The first time my father returned from sea and my mother slept in a room she rented across town, I missed her with a force so terrible it made me sick. My longing felt like a disintegration of self, or a distillation of self—everything concentrated into a single panicked obsession. My toys were drained of all their pleasure. No story could rescue me. To protect my father, whose heart was also broken and who I loved equally but depended upon less, I hid my despair. In secret, I called my mother on the telephone and cried. I had never been apart from her. I hadn't known that she was my home.

My birthday falls during Pyanepsion, the fourth month of the ancient Greek calendar. It is the month of Persephone's abduction, the month Demeter's despair laid all the earth to waste, and during which the women of Athens celebrated the

Thesmophoria—a fertility festival that lasted three days, each with its own title: Kathodos, Nēsteia, and Kalligeneia. The rites of the Thesmophoria were kept secret from men and included the burying of sacrifices and the retrieval of the previous year's oblations—often the bodies of slain pigs— whose remains were offered on altars to the goddesses and then scattered in the fields with the year's seeds.

When I got my first period at thirteen, my mother wanted to have a party. "Just small, all women," she said. "I want to celebrate you." It was already too late. I seethed with something greater than the advent of my own fertility, the hormones catapulting through my body, the fact of our severed family, or the end of my child form. I'd been taught by my mother to honor these changes, but there were things for which she could not prepare me. The sum of it all was unspeakable. I would rather have died than celebrate this metamorphosis with her. It is so painful to be loved sometimes. Intolerable, even.

Psychologists and philosophers have numerous explanations for the anger that attends this cleaving between parents and children. I have read about separation and differentiation and individuation. It is a most ordinary disruption, necessarily awful, sometimes severe—especially for mothers and daughters. The closer the mother and the daughter are, the more violent the daughter's effort to disentangle herself can be. I'm not looking for permission or assurance that ours was a normal break; rather, a different kind of understanding. For that, I need to retell our story.

I imagine myself as my mother—which is to say, a lover, and my beloved as someone with whom I spend twelve years of uninterrupted, undifferentiated intimacy. It is an affair in which the burden of responsibility, of care, lies solely upon me. I imagine, also, simultaneous duties, now seemingly less important since my child's arrival: in Demeter's case, the earth's fertility, the nourishment of all its people, and the cycle of life and death. After twelve years, my beloved rejects me. She does not leave. She does not cease to depend on me—I still must clothe and feed her, ferry her through each day, attend to her health, and occasionally offer her comfort. Mostly, though, she becomes unwilling to accept my tenderness. She exiles me from her interior world almost entirely. She is furious. She is clearly in pain and possibly in danger. Every step I take toward her, she backs further away.

Of course, this is a flawed analogy. I turn to it because we have so many narratives to make sense of romantic love, sexual love, marriage, but none that feel adequate to both the heartbreak my mother must have felt and the kinds of love I have known since. The attachment styles that define our adult relationships are determined in that first emotional connection with our parents, aren't they? More than a few times I have felt the shock of losing access to a lover; it doesn't matter who leaves. It feels like a crime against nature, a kind of torture, to be robbed of that presence. It must have been thus for my mother—for Demeter, as she watched Persephone be carried away in that black chariot, and then the earth broke open to swallow her.

2. *Nēsteia*

Cape Cod, April. I was thirteen and had spent that Saturday at the library with Stacy. At least, that was what I had told my mother when I got in her car that evening. The sun was half sunk behind a cluster of storefronts, the afternoon's warmth had turned cool, a breeze from the nearby harbor carrying the soft clang of a buoy's bell. I buckled my seat belt and waved goodbye to Stacy, who turned to walk home. My mother and I watched her stiff, straight-backed gait, the edge of her T-shirt rippling in the wind. She did walk a little bit like a robot, as Ben had observed when she left us in his room together, and then he fumbled in my underwear.

"You smell like sex," my mother said. Her tone was one of exhaustion. *Please*, it said, *just tell me the truth. I know it already. Let's be in this together.*

It was easy to present the shock of my humiliation and incredulity. I'd done so before, and we both knew it.

"I've never had sex," I said. I believed this.

My mother shifted into gear and turned toward the exit. "Sex isn't just intercourse," she said.

We drove home in silence. I don't know if we had a conversation about trust that night. We'd had them so many times before, my mother trying to broker an understanding, to cast a single line across the distance between us. If trust was broken, my mother explained, it had to be rebuilt. But the sanctity of our trust held no currency with me, so broken trust came to mean the loss of certain freedoms. She didn't want to revoke my privileges; she wanted me to come home to her. Probably I knew this. If she didn't like the distance my lies created, then she would like even less my silence and sulks, my slammed bedroom door. Of course I won these battles. We each had something the other wanted, but I alone had conviction.

How many times could she call me a liar, or believe me to be one? I was relentless in my refusal to acknowledge what we both knew. I went on drug deliveries with a friend's mother who sold them, snuck boys into our home or met them behind the movie theater. Grown men groped me in backyards and basements, on docks and in doorways, and there was nothing my mother could do to protect me.

The Rape of Persephone is depicted by hundreds of artists, across thousands of years. In epic poetry the word *rape* is often translated as a synonym for abduction to temper its violence. In most sculpture, Persephone writhes in the arms of Hades, torquing her soft body away from his muscled arms and enormous legs. Consider Gian Lorenzo Bernini's famous Baroque version, in which Hades's fingers press into her thighs and waist. The white stone is so yielding as to seem fleshlike, Persephone's arms fully extended while her hands push against his face and head. In Rembrandt's *Rape of Proserpina*, as Hades's chariot plunges through foaming water into darkness and the Oceanids cling to her satin skirts, he grasps Persephone's leg and pulls her into his pelvis. Her gown hides the rest.

My mother surely feared that I would be raped. It was a legitimate concern. In hindsight I am surprised it never happened. Perhaps because I feared it as much as she did. Or because I so often yielded to or negotiated with those who would have otherwise forced themselves on me.

It must have felt like an abduction to my mother, as if someone had stolen her daughter and replaced her with a harpy. I chose to leave her, to lie, to rush to places where men might lay their hands on me, but I was still a child. Who, then, was my abductor? Can we call it Hades, the desire that filled me like smoke, that chased everything else out? I was frightened, yes, but I went willingly. Perhaps that was the scariest part.

In *Eros the Bittersweet*, Anne Carson explores the term *poikilos nomos*—given in Plato's *Symposium* to describe a "contradictory ethic" in which upper-class men were encouraged to fall in love with beautiful boys who spurned their pursuit. While *nomos* means law or convention, "*poikilos* is an adjective applicable to anything variegated, complex or shifting"; "This erotic code," Carson tells us, "is a social expression of the division within a lover's heart."

A convention of Spartan weddings widely adopted across Greece was for a groom to seize his writhing bride across his body and "abduct" her by chariot, in a seemingly perfect simulacrum of Persephone's rape.

"The Athenian *nomos* is *poikilos*," writes Carson, "in that it recommends an ambivalent code of behavior . . . But the *nomos* is also *poikilos* in that it applies to a phenomenon whose essence and loveliness is *in* its ambivalence."

We all know the allure of the reluctant lover. But what of our own divided hearts? My ambivalence tormented and compelled me. That *eros* was an engine that hummed in me, propelled me away from our home into the darkness. I knew it was dangerous. I couldn't tell the difference between my fear and desire—both thrilled my body, itself already a stranger to me. There was a *nomos* for this. Daughters were supposed to leave their mothers, to grope for the bulging shapes of men and then resist them. My mother must have anticipated this, must have hoped she would be spared.

Wasn't my mother also my beloved, my captor? If *eros* is lack, then it existed between us. Wasn't it against her arms that I fought most viciously? Like the Spartan bride, I would have lost my heart if she had truly let me go. A daughter is wedded to her mother first.

In the "Hymn to Demeter," the Homeric poet tells that "for nine days did the Lady Demeter / wander all over the earth, holding torches ablaze in her hands." After that, she takes a human form and becomes the caretaker of an Eleusinian boy, who she tries and fails to make immortal.

When I was thirteen, my mother went back to school to become a psychotherapist. She rode a Greyhound bus to Boston each week for class, textbooks propped on her lap. The job of a therapist is not so different from a mother's, although it is safer. It is collaboration and care, but not symbiosis. It is not reciprocal in its need. Her patients may have been the Eleusinian children who could never be made immortal, but she did not set them on fire as Demeter did that boy. She helped them as I would not allow myself to be helped.

When I told her, just a few months short of seventeen, that I was moving out, she didn't try to stop me. I knew she didn't want me to go. "Maybe I should have tried to stop you," she has said to me more than once. "But I was afraid that I would lose you for good."

Zeus insisted Hades return Persephone to her mother, and the dark lord capitulated, on one condition: if Persephone had tasted any food of the underworld, she would be consigned to return to Hades for half of every year. Did Persephone know? Yes and no. In some versions, she thinks she is smart enough to evade him, to taste and still go home. There are so many holes in the myth, so many versions and mutations, most unstamped by chronology. A myth is the memory of a story passed through time. Like any memory, it changes. Sometimes by will, or necessity, or forgetting, or even for aesthetic purpose.

The pomegranate seeds were so lovely, like rubies, and so sweet. In every version of the story, Persephone tastes them.

It was winter in Boston. I was seventeen. I didn't start with heroin. I started with meth, though we called it crystal, which sounded much prettier than the burnt clumps of tinfoil that littered our apartment and whose singed smell hung in the air, as if an oven had been left on too long.

Imagine Persephone's first season in hell. When I phoned home, I apologized to my mother for not calling. "I've been busy with classes. I'm making such nice friends."

These were half-truths. I wasn't missing classes. I did make friends. I had a job and homework and a bedroom without a door that cost me $150 per month in rent. My mother would have paid for more, but with it she would have also bought more claim on the truth.

When I rode that same Greyhound bus home and ate the meals she made and slept in my old room, it *was* like rising from some underworld to the golden light of earth. I missed it so much. I couldn't wait to leave.

Imagine Persephone loving Hades. Is it so impossible? She could not have escaped him by dying, after all. We often love the things that abduct us. I imagine I would find a way, if I were bound to someone for the rest of my life—for half of eternity.

It was Christmas or Thanksgiving. My mother, brother, and I joined hands around the table, the steaming food encircled by our arms. We squeezed each other's fingers, pressed our thumbs into each other's palms. That small triad, who had been so sad and strong and fiercely loving.

After the dishes were washed, my mother sank into the sofa and smiled at us. "Should we play a game?" she asked. "Watch a movie?"

"I need to borrow your car," I said.

I can hardly bear to remember her disappointed face.

"Where could you possibly have to go tonight?"

I don't remember what I answered, only that she let me and how much it hurt to leave them. I pulled the front door shut behind me, and something tore inside, like a chapped lip that rends at a word. Still, the quickening as I lit a cigarette in the dark and turned off our road toward the highway. I imagine that this is the way a man feels, leaving his family for his mistress. I did feel part father, part husband, and maybe every daughter does. Or just the ones whose fathers are gone.

I didn't tell her when I got clean. She'd never known I started. She knew what she saw, and that was bad enough. You can't crawl up to your mother from hell and not look like it. If I told her why she didn't have to worry anymore, I'd have to confirm why she'd worried. I'd have to be done for good. What if Persephone had told Demeter not only what happened in hell, but that she *might* be coming home for good? What daughter would do that?

Another holiday. After dinner, all of us draped over the couch, drowsy with food.

"I need to borrow your car," I said.

Her pleading face. "Where could you possibly be going?"

I took a breath. "I have to go to a meeting," I said. Then I had to explain. "Things have been bad."

She wanted to know how bad. Or thought she did.

I revealed very little. As she listened, her expression grew tired. "It all makes so much more sense now," she said, wearily.

I wanted to take it all back. How much are you supposed to tell someone who loves you that much, who you want to protect? Is it worse for them to find out later, when you're safely on the other side? I hated to watch my mother sort through the past, solving the puzzle of my inconsistencies with the pieces I'd withheld. Lies make fools of the people we love. It's a careful equation, protecting them at the cost of your betrayal. Like mortgaging the house again to pay for the car. I was also always protecting myself. There were things I would no longer be able to believe if I had to say them aloud. I could only tell her the truth when I faced it.

Three years later, I sent her the book I'd written.

"You can't call me until you've finished reading it," I said. In it were all the things I'd never told her, or anyone. "Take as much time as you need," I said, hoping that she'd take long enough to *not* need to talk to me about how it felt to know those things.

She agreed.

The phone rang the next morning at seven o'clock.

"I couldn't stop reading it," she said. "I kept putting it down and turning out the light and then turning it back on and picking up the book again."

When I asked what she found so riveting about it, she said, "I had to know you were going to be all right.

"It was the hardest thing I've ever had to read," she said. "It's wonderful."

In the years that followed, she sometimes told me about the awkward things her colleagues said to her about the book, the ways she had to explain my past and the ways she couldn't.

"I've had my own experience of it," she once said. I knew she meant that she wanted me to make room for how it had been hard for her, too—the living *and* the telling. I had made a choice to tell the world the things I couldn't talk about. In doing so, I had forced myself to talk about them, though I still barely could with her. My choice revealed those things to her and simultaneously forced her to have a conversation with the world. Even more unfair, I didn't want to know about it. I couldn't bear to listen.

Five years after I sent my mother that book, I had a lover who wanted me to always be thinking of her. When I was, she lavished me with gifts and grand gestures of affection. When I wasn't, she punished me, mostly by withdrawing. At this, I felt a touch of that old disintegration, that sickened longing. It was a torment—a compelling cycle to which I consented.

The first time I brought her home to meet my mother, she only looked at me. At dinner, she answered my mother's questions but did not ask any. Her eyes sought mine as if tending something there. It was hard for me to look anywhere else.

"She's so focused on you," my mother said. "It's odd." I could tell she was being generous.

My lover had brought a gift for my mother, a necklace made of lavender beads, smooth as the inside of a mussel shell. In the bedroom, she removed the small box from her suitcase and handed it to me.

"Give it to her," my lover said.

"But it's from you," I said.

"It's better if you give it to her," she said.

I knew that my mother would also find this odd, just like her need to be alone with me so much during such a short visit.

"We'll give it to her together," I said.

In the months after I left her, it was tempting to interpret this behavior as an expression of my lover's guilty conscience, but I don't think she knew enough about herself to feel guilty in front of my mother. More likely, she saw my mother as a competitor. I suspect that she feared my mother would see something in her that I couldn't yet. Still, for the two years we were together I withdrew from my mother almost entirely. I could not see what was happening to me and didn't want to. Like my lover, I refused to look at my mother. I didn't want to see what she saw.

A few times, I called her, sobbing. I'd also done this when I was on heroin.

"Do you think I'm a good person?" I asked.

"Of course," she said and I could hear her brow's furrow. I could feel how much she still wanted to help me. I hung up the phone. I missed her so much, worse than ever before. *Please come get me*, I wanted to say, as I had when I was a child. This time, there was no way for her to bring me home.

The morning that I finally decided to leave the relationship, I called my mother. This time, I didn't wait three years to write a book about it and then send it to her.

"I'm leaving her," I said. "It's been so much worse than I told you."

"How?" she asked. After I revealed everything, she wanted to know why I hadn't confided in her.

"I don't know," I said. I was weeping. "What if I'd told you and then didn't leave her?"

She was quiet for a moment. "Did you think that I would hold that against you?"

I wept harder and covered my eyes with my hand.

"Listen to me," she said, her voice as firm as a hand under my chin. "You could never lose me. I will love you every day of your life."

When I didn't answer, she said, "Do you hear me? There is nothing you could do to make me stop loving you."

3. Kalligeneia

When I sent my second book to my mother, we had an hours-long conversation. I explained how my writing created a place where I could look at and talk to parts of myself that I otherwise couldn't. She explained to me that this was exactly what her mode of therapy allowed her patients to do. We had talked about this before, but never in such depth.

A few months later, at a conference my mother attends every year, we stood in front of a room packed with therapists. She began the workshop by leading them through an explanation of the model she trains clinicians in around the world. She was warm and funny, expert and charismatic. You could easily see why our mailbox filled with heartfelt cards from patients she'd stopped seeing decades ago. When she was done, I stood and spoke about how writing allows me to retread the most painful parts of the past and find not only new meaning but also healing there. Then I led the audience through a writing exercise that exemplified this and drew upon my mother's therapy model. Afterward I invited a few of the therapists to share their work. As they read, the group nodded and laughed. A few people wept.

That whole weekend, people clasped our hands and praised our work together. They marveled at the miracle of our collaboration. "How special," they said. "Whose idea was this?"

"Hers," I told them.

As the memories of stories are changed with each telling, they are more irrevocably changed with each conquest, each colonizer, each assimilation of one people into another. There are older versions of Demeter's story, precursors to the Greek, that emerged from a system of matrifocal mythology and likely a society whose values it reflected.

There was no rape, no abduction. The mother, goddess of the cycle of life and death, passed freely from underworld to earth, receiving those who died as they passed from one to the next. Her daughter, some of these older versions say, was simply the maiden version of that goddess, imbued with the same powers. Others suggest that Persephone was the very old goddess of the underworld, and always had been.

It used to scare me that I wanted things my mother wouldn't understand. I think we both feared our difference. In hiding it from her, I often created exactly the thing I wished to avoid. It's not that I should have told her everything; that would have been its own kind of cruelty, though I could have trusted her more. That younger version of our story, the one I've carried for most of my life, the one I've mostly told of here, is also true: I hurt myself and I hurt her, over and over. But like the matrifocal myth, there is another version, a wiser one.

In it, Persephone is already home. Her time spent in the dark is not an aberration of nature but its enactment. I've come to see mine the same way. My darkness has become my work on this earth. I return to my mother again and again, and both realms are my home. There is no Hades, no abductor. There is only me. There is nothing down there that I haven't found a piece of in myself. I am glad to have learned that I do not have to hide this from her. It helps that the darkness is now less likely than ever to kill me.

I can hold both of these stories inside me. There is room for one in the other. The first myth of mother and daughter I sacrifice on the first day of the Thesmophoria, Kathodos, a ritual violence. The other, I retrieve on the third day, Kalligeneia, and sprinkle in the fields. All of my violences might be seen this way: a descent, a rise, a sowing. If we sow them, every sacrifice becomes a harvest.

As the Rome traffic heaved outside the window of that tiny apartment, I stared at my phone while dread thickened in me. I understood that I could sink this whole trip into it, spend every day punishing myself for my mistake. I didn't have to, though. The part of me who feared the bond between my mother and me too fragile to withstand this blow was a younger self. I had to tell her about this new story, that there was nothing I could do that would make my mother stop loving me. I promised her. Then, I called my mother.

She was mad, of course, and disappointed, but by the end of the call we were laughing.

A few days later I phoned her from the town where her grandmother was born.

"You are going to love it here," I said.

There is a difference between the fear of upsetting someone who loves you and the danger of losing them. For a long time, I couldn't separate these. It has taken me some work to discern the difference between the pain of hurting those I love and my fear of what I might lose. Hurting those we love is survivable. It is inevitable. I wish that I could have done less of it.

A year later I picked my mother up at the Naples airport and we drove down the coast to that town, Vico Equense. For two weeks, we ate fresh tomatoes and mozzarella and walked the same streets that her grandmother had. I drove us down the entire Amalfi coast and only scratched the rental car a little.

As I drove, my mother held my phone up to film the shocking blue waters that rippled below, the sheer drop from the highway's edge, the wheeling birds that seemed to follow us, and the tiny villages built into the hillside. It was terrifying and beautiful, like all my favorite journeys.

Back home the following week, I sort through the pictures, deleting doubles and smiling at our happy faces. When I get to that video and play it, I see an image of her sandaled foot—wide like my own—on the gritty floor of our rented Fiat. Our voices, recorded with perfect clarity, comment on the scenery. She is holding the phone's camera upside down, I realize, while the GPS map fills the display. I snort and continue watching her foot shift as our voices remark on a passing bus. Then, alone at my desk in Brooklyn, I close my eyes and listen to our conversation rippling eagerly through time, our gasps as mopeds speed by us on hairpin turns, and our laughter ringing on and on.

It is the thing I have been
trying to undo in myself
and it has been a life's work.

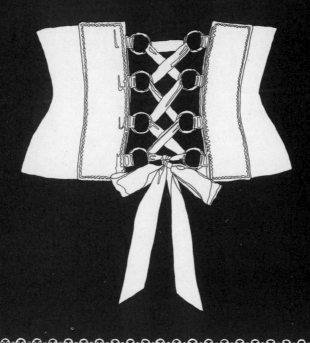

THANK YOU FOR TAKING CARE
OF YOURSELF

In a series of famously sadistic experiments conducted throughout the 1960s, Harry Harlow isolated infant rhesus monkeys and deprived them of touch for up to a full year. Harlow was interested in reproducing the human experience of depression in his monkeys, and at this he succeeded, surprising no one. After thirty days, isolated monkeys were assessed as "enormously disturbed," and those isolated for longer periods displayed "severe deficits in virtually every aspect of social behavior," weakened immune systems, overproduction of stress hormones, inability to have sexual relations, and tendencies to self-harm and starve themselves. Monkeys isolated for a full year were largely incapable of rehabilitation.

His results are reproduced each year by the estimated eighty thousand American prison inmates held in solitary confinement, and on a smaller scale, by the immeasurable number of people who live in societies that discourage regular forms of touch, like ours. Psychologists call it "skin hunger" and posit that many experiences of depression are actually symptoms of touch deprivation.

I have been reading about Harry Harlow and skin hunger since my friend Mairo sent me an e-mail with the subject heading "this seems like something you'd be interested in" and a link to something called a "cuddle party." I followed the link to a website and immediately rolled my eyes. I did not suffer from skin hunger. In fact, I had spent most of the year before I met my girlfriend intentionally celibate, during which time I experienced very little touch aside from that of my chiropractor. Those months had arguably been the best of my life. Nonetheless, my interest was piqued. The immediacy of my aversion to the cuddle party made me curious. As the people we hate on sight are usually those in whom we recognize ourselves and no one more dismissive of sobriety than the alcoholic, knee-jerk repulsion is a kind of metal detector. Experience has taught me that when such an alarm sounds, there is usually something buried nearby.

"Would you be comfortable with my attending something called a cuddle party?" I asked Donika. While I had been luxuriating in my voluntary respite from touch in New York City, my girlfriend then lived in western New York State, one hundred miles from the nearest city. That is, in a location known for its long and bitter winters and so remote that few friends came to visit her. Most of her days there passed without her seeing a single other Black person or getting a hug.

"Absolutely," she said without hesitation. "Would you be comfortable with my joining you?"

Cuddle Party was founded by Reid Mihalko and Marcia Baczynski in 2004 and incorporated in 2016. Over the last fourteen years, they have hosted cuddle parties across the United States and internationally, and trained over two hundred professional cuddlers to meet the needs of the touch-deprived. Similar organizations have sprung up, like Cuddle Sanctuary in Los Angeles, and Cuddlist in New York City.

In the days leading up to the event, I read copious articles and scoured the official Cuddle Party website, which was designed with the obvious questions in mind. The rules for cuddle parties are prominently listed and focused on consent and a clear boundary between sexual and nonsexual touching. Attendees are instructed to wear full pajamas, and touching in any "bikini areas" is prohibited. Part of their stated mission is to differentiate between sex and cuddling and to offer access to healthy touch that isn't confused with sex. All of this seemed appealing to me in the abstract, if not personally.

During the years in my early twenties when I worked as a pro-domme, the sessions in which a client wanted some form of tenderness or sensuality were just as common as the ones that included insults. My clients were often profoundly lonely men. They were often trauma survivors. I have no doubt that a significant percentage suffered from skin hunger. It sometimes felt to me as though their skin was a tapestry of invisible mouths, all clamoring to be fed.

In my first year on the job, I preferred the sessions in which a client wanted to be held or tended to with affection rather than corporal punishment or humiliation, because I already knew how to perform that service. Over time, my comfort with more sensual sessions became distaste, and then my distaste became disgust, and finally my disgust became loathing. To enact tenderness felt like a greater betrayal of self than any act of violence and many sexual acts. To let those needy, entitled strangers into a space—both physical and metaphysical—reserved for people I loved would contaminate it. I instinctually understood that I could not let them in, or else the meaning of those actions would change for me. So I locked them out. That is, I detached myself from the experience. It may be more accurate to say that I locked myself in. I took the part of me that screamed at their touch, and I put her away where I could not hear her. I dimmed the lights in the house of myself and locked the bedroom doors.

Later, when people asked me what I felt during these sessions, I answered honestly: "Nothing."

I don't refer to any of my experiences in sex work as traumatic because it is an inexact description, and the assumptions that such a statement prompts in the minds of others are incorrect. Trauma, especially in the context of sex work, is associated with victimhood. Unlike many of the world's sex workers, I did not have sex work forced upon me by another person or circumstance. Etymologically, the word *trauma* originates from the Greek word for "wound," and that is typically how we use it today, to describe both physical and metaphysical wounds. My experiences in sex work were not wounding per se, though the longitudinal effects that I have observed in myself do overlap some—in their tenacity and their affect—with those of people who have been wounded. I have had to think closely about this because much of how I understand trauma is as an event that changes a person, or for which a person changes herself, in order to withstand—an event that redraws the psychic or emotional map in some lasting way that later proves inhibitive. All of these do describe my experience with sex work. That starting place, however, that initial *wounding*, the connotation of victimization—I can't align my own experience with it. I have often wished for a different word, one that implies profound, often inhibitive, change, but precludes the wound and victimization inherent in *trauma*, which has become such a charged and overused term outside its clinical definition. For now, I will use *event*, a word whose etymology suggests consequences rather than wounds. I am not interested in defining my experiences as wounds so much as in examining their consequences.

I do imagine that this dimming, this voluntary dissociation, produced a similar effect on my brain as on those of trauma survivors. In a brain scan of a patient experiencing this detachment—referred to in extreme cases as "depersonalization"—the brain is an empty field, marred only by pixelated blemishes here and there. There is dramatically decreased activity in every area, and the dissociated person's thoughts slow like a spoon in thickening paste. One woman I later interviewed called it "that frozen feeling." It is often described as an out-of-body feeling, the sense of a consciousness detached from the corporeal self, perhaps watching it as one would a figure in a diorama. Which is exactly why it is so effective as a survival mechanism. The frozen self doesn't feel the affect of that self, though it is recorded in the body. The body, it turns out, is an abacus that never forgets, even when our memories do.

That detachment only worked for a time. By my third year, I could hardly stand for my clients to touch me at all. Toward the end of my time in the job, I remember seeing a regular who used to come for a thirty-minute session every week or two and ask me to massage his legs for the whole half hour. Sometimes, with his taut, bristly calves in my hands, I would startle awake inside myself and fill with a rage so seething I'd have to leave the room.

I wasn't thinking of any of this when I went to the cuddle party.

I drove Donika, Mairo, and myself from Brooklyn to the Upper East Side on a Saturday afternoon. It was springtime. Mairo had agreed to join us, though she expressed the most emphatic skepticism.

"I mean, who are these people?" she said from the back seat as we cruised up Third Avenue. "I can't believe I agreed to this."

We arrived at the address and were buzzed into what, in the RSVP e-mail, had been called "Holistic Loft." At the top of a narrow stairway slumped rows of discarded shoes. We slid ours off and pushed open the cracked door. Inside was a crush of people, including a man who took our names and checked them off a list. "I'm Adam," he said, and I recognized him as the founder of Cuddlist. For $25 we had reserved our first-come first-serve tickets, which had quickly sold out.

A few sock-footed people waited in line for the restroom, and two others held up a sheet in the small kitchen area while a third person changed into their pajamas behind it. Having worn our pajamas to the party, we inched our way through this small hubbub and into the open space of the loft. My first impression was that it was mostly men, about two-thirds. I suspected that, as with coed sex parties (of which I'd attended only a couple in my early twenties, but in whose vicinity I had circulated for years) and many nightclubs, there was a regular surplus of eager men, and the organizers had to strategize their appeal to women. I figured that the three of us were a welcome sight, a hunch confirmed by the stares as we navigated the room. It made me a little nervous, as if we'd just stepped onto the altar of lonely men.

The loft had been arranged as an enormous bed, the floor laid with wide cushions, blankets, pillows, and low couches against the wall. The late-afternoon light spilled in through two windows on whose sills sat an assortment of crystals.

The three of us picked our way to a clearing on the floor and carefully settled. The age range of the group seemed to span from folks in their twenties through those in their fifties. A young man with a nervous, handsome face sat nearby, as well as a man and a woman who looked to be in their thirties and were already cuddling—the woman leaned back against the man, his arm intimately wrapped around her torso. The sensual nature of their touch seemed at odds with the tone of the cuddle party, and I assumed they were a couple. My girlfriend and I had agreed beforehand not to cuddle with one another—primarily because that seemed to defeat the purpose of attending the party, and secondarily, because we didn't want to risk violating the platonic rule. This couple seemed less conscientious. The woman wore a skimpy pair of shorts with a T-shirt, despite what the website and e-mails to attendees had advised: "Sweats are fine, but no shorts or tank tops, please. Think less lace, more flannel. No lingerie." When the woman introduced herself to me, her friendliness seemed both suggestive and performative. It was her first cuddle party, she said. The swingerish energy that she and her partner emanated was familiar to me. It reminded me of the couples I would sometimes see as a domme. Women never came in for sessions alone, and when couples did, it was almost always the man's idea. I leaned away from them.

The nervous young man and I smiled politely at one another and introduced ourselves. It was his first time as well. Across the floor I saw a man about my age in a teal onesie—like adult-size footie pajamas—stroking the arm of a jovial blond woman in fleece pants and a worn T-shirt. Unlike the couple, they seemed at ease, platonic, regulars to the cuddle party. A number of men sat awkwardly not talking to anyone. The regulars were easier to pick out—they chatted and embraced one another, and cheerfully introduced themselves to the loners. It was a very white space. There appeared to be even fewer people of color than there were women. Aside from my companions—both Black women—there seemed fewer than five other people of color among the thirty or so attendees.

Soon Adam gathered us in a circle that covered the entire perimeter of the room. He spoke in a warm tone as he reviewed the rules of the cuddle party. These had been emailed to all attendees prior to the party as follows:

1. Pajamas stay on the whole time.
2. You don't have to cuddle anyone at a Cuddle Party, ever.
3. You must ask permission and receive a verbal YES before you touch anyone. (Be as specific in your request as you can.)
4. If you're a yes, say YES. If you're a no, say NO.
5. If you're a maybe, say NO.
6. You are encouraged to change your mind.
7. Respect your relationship agreements and communicate with your partner.
8. Get your Cuddle Party Facilitator or the Cuddle Assistant if you have a question or concern or need assistance with anything during the Cuddle Party.
9. Tears and laughter are both welcome.

10. Respect people's privacy when sharing about Cuddle Parties.

11. Keep the Cuddle space tidy

Some of these seemed more obvious, such as "Pajamas stay on at all times" and "Respect people's privacy when sharing about Cuddle Parties." Others, while comprehensible, were sentiments I'd never seen before, like "You are encouraged to change your mind." I had reviewed all of the rules before deciding to attend and been heartened by the emphasis on consent, but that emphasis was even more pronounced in practice.

Adam acknowledged how difficult it can be to establish clear boundaries around touch. Many of us, he said, did not learn how to say no in our families, or how to differentiate between different kinds of touch. When we got to rule 3, "You must ask permission and receive a verbal YES before you touch anyone," he asked us to turn to a nearby person and perform a role-play. One person was to ask, "Do you want to cuddle?" The other was to answer, "No." The first would then respond, "Thank you for taking care of yourself."

The young man and I faced one another.

"Do you want to cuddle?" he asked.

"No," I said, and my mouth involuntarily stretched into a smile, as if I needed to soften the refusal. My face grew hot, and I felt myself blinking quickly. Was it really so hard for me to give an anticipated no? I felt uneasy in my body, surprised by the strength of my reaction to the exercise.

Next, Adam asked us to repeat the role-play, but this time to ask our partners, "Can I kiss you?" Kissing is not allowed at the cuddle party, so this exercise was even more moot than the previous one. Still, I had no interest whatsoever in kissing the young man, and to feign one, even in this transparent context, increased my discomfort exponentially. I understood that to pretend a sexual interest was a greater compromise for me than it was for him. A woman's sexual invitation carries implications that felt dangerous even in this prescribed simulation. My voice croaked when I asked, and his face flushed when he said no. When he asked me and I refused him again, my tone was so apologetic that it seemed farcical. I couldn't seem to control my affect; like a pinched hose, the words eked out of me in odd directions. I was relieved when we turned back toward Adam to continue our study of the rules.

The emphasis on not simply consent but *enthusiastic* consent was heartening. I thought of myself as someone fluent in the contemporary dialogue around consent. But this was the first space outside of a monogamous relationship that I'd encountered where my own enthusiastic consent was encouraged and where I was encouraged to change my mind. BDSM culture similarly emphasizes ongoing enthusiastic consent and clearly delineated boundaries, but my experience was in the commercial realm of BDSM; while there had been things I wouldn't ever do, for the most part my clients paid for my consent and the illusion of its enthusiasm.

By the time we finished the orientation portion of the cuddle party, I would have been happy to leave. I had no desire to cuddle with anyone and felt exhausted by the role-play. A soundtrack of instrumental spa music played as people crawled around the soft floor and entwined. The man in the teal onesie crawled over to me. He was handsome, with olive skin and hazel eyes, and disconcertingly infantilized by the onesie. I had no particular feeling about him. He was just a man.

"Hi," he said affably. "Would you like to spoon with me?"

"Sure," I said. I did not hesitate to assess if I really wanted to spoon with him. I had no lucid thought about it at all. I simply agreed, and we settled on the chenille-blanketed floor. He curled around me as the big spoon. I did not think: I do not want this man's body curled around me. My uneasiness did not occur as a thought at all. It was more like a shift in temperature, a change in the light, a texture inside me that roughened.

"Can I rub your arm?" he asked.

I nodded my assent. I did not think of the cuddle party's requirement of verbal consent. His body was warm against

mine, and his touch didn't wander from my upper arm. I felt
the nubs on the sleeve of his onesie rub against my bare skin.
I wondered what my girlfriend was doing, if she was similarly
spooned with some warm stranger, if it felt good to her.
I wondered how long I needed to remain in this position to
avoid seeming rude. To describe the way that I felt as a "maybe"
would be generous, but I did not think of rule 5: "If you're a
maybe, say no." I did not feel "encouraged to change my mind."
That is, whatever the culture of the cuddle party, the culture
inside me presented its own dictates. It was not the warmly
lit Holistic Loft of my late thirties. It was a twilit space in
which thoughts moved like half-remembered dreams. It was
a hallway with a closed door at the end. In it, I was half stranger.

"Can I join you guys?" asked a woman's voice. I looked up to
see the woman from the swingerish couple kneeling over us.

"Fine with me," sang my big spoon. She didn't wait for me
to answer, but scooted up behind him. Sandwiched between
us, my big spoon sighed with contentment. I felt his breath
on my hair and began to study the blanket under me, whose
lavender fabric looked exhausted. I wondered how often the
bedding was laundered.

When the woman's hand slipped over his waist and began
to stroke mine, I felt confused. First, about who was touching
me, and second, about why it felt so wrong. She hadn't asked,
I realized. Her touch seemed to vibrate with the same quality

as her voice. There was something unhinged about her performative openness, the current of sexual suggestion that flowed from her. I had been such a performer as a younger woman. I knew that that sort of act was inherently ironic: the actual meaning was the opposite of what it expressed. The true desires of such performers are hidden, sometimes even from themselves, and this detachment renders them unreliable communicators of their own consent and unreliable detectors of others'. As she touched me, I recognized all of this—not in thoughts, but in my body's instinctive revulsion. Then I finally had the thought: I don't have to do this.

I broke away, smiling. "I'm going to wander around," I told them, and crept into the kitchen. If I could have shaken my entire body to release the tension that had accumulated, like a dog after a bath, I would have. Instead, I walked into the small kitchen and grazed from an assortment of silver bowls that held baby carrots, almonds, and squares of chocolate. I stood alone in the kitchen area and looked out at the landscape of cuddlers. They reminded me of the prairie dogs I'd once observed in an exhibit at the Arizona-Sonora Desert Museum, which cuddled together in soft clusters, or stood leaning into one another, seeming always to prefer touching to not touching.

When Adam warned the group that there were only twenty minutes left, I took a deep breath. One cuddle was not enough to *experience* the cuddle party, was it? My companions looked so contented. Perhaps I had simply begun with some incompatible partners. I gingerly ventured back onto the floor and took a seat near the wall. The young man with whom I'd role-played during the orientation workshop quickly found me and stiffly asked if I'd like to cuddle. I smiled at him and made a noncommittal sound, as though a breeze were slipping through a cracked window in me.

"What sort of cuddling?" I asked.

"Like that?" he said, and indicated a pair nearby, entwined face-to-face, one's leg thrown over the other's hip.

The *no* rung like a gong in me. A ripple of panic followed. "How about something a little . . . lighter," I suggested. As I spoke, I felt my face scrunch into a grimace, as if I, too, were disappointed that I did not want to entwine with this stranger.

Despite his obvious nerves, I detected a note of annoyance when he said, "Like what?"

"Hand-holding?" I offered. I could not control my face.

"How about I massage your shoulders?" he countered.

I nodded. He sat behind me, the heat and tension of his body cast like a shadow over my back. I tried not to lean away from him. For a few minutes his hands fumbled inexpertly at my shoulders. I could feel their clamminess through my cotton shirt. When Adam announced that we should begin regathering for a closing circle, I pulled away and smiled at my abysmal masseur.

The attendees slowly crawled into formation, encircling the space, bodies looser, cheeks aglow, very much as if their hungry skin had been heartily fed. They leaned together and in some cases remained entangled even as we all held hands. Adam led us through a brief meditation and invited people to share a few words about their experience.

"Wonderful!" someone shouted and was answered by gentle laughter.

When the closing circle ended, and Donika returned from the other side of the room, I wrapped my arms around her waist and burrowed into her like a child, as if her touch were a corrective that I badly needed.

"Hi, friend," she said, and kissed my forehead.

The three of us slipped out the door before the rush and found our shoes in the pile on the landing. As we descended the narrow staircase, a wave of giddy relief washed over me.

It had grown dark outside. As I drove us back to Brooklyn, the lights of restaurants and delis on Third Avenue glided over our faces, and I listened to my companions recount the pleasures of their experience. Mairo had surprised herself at her readiness to cuddle, and her laughter was shy but happy as we gently teased her. Donika, too, seemed easy with the success of her cuddling. She had remained with the same woman for nearly the entire cuddling portion of the party. Neither she nor Mairo exhibited any trace of the sticky web of feelings that still ensnared me. As I listened to them and observed the dramatic difference between our experiences, I grew quieter. There was something—a touch of shame or embarrassment—that arose in me.

"That was exactly what I wanted," said Donika. "How about you, sweetie?"

"I don't know," I said slowly. I tried to explain the feeling I'd had in that room. I had only been half cognizant of it in the loft, but even with this short hindsight it came into focus. The particular combination of desperation, loneliness, and entitlement that some of the men at the cuddle party had exuded struck me the way an ex's perfume on the neck of a passing stranger can. They were so vulnerable, and there was also a coldness in them. Desperation can be a profoundly self-centered state. The desperate do not necessarily see the world and its other people with the easy detachment of the contented. They have a heightened sense of potential resources. My past had taught me that the devotion of the needy—which I had known from both sides—while complete, is not always loving. There can be a mercenary quality to it.

"It was like being in a room scattered with my clients when I was a domme," I told them.

"Except you weren't getting paid?" said Mairo with a rueful chuckle.

It went deeper than that. They reminded me of my birth father, a career alcoholic I'd only met in my thirties and who had died shortly after. For the few months we knew each other, he'd acted as if he wanted to forge an emotional connection that I had no interest in. I suspect that what he actually wanted was money.

My friends had also recognized the pitiful quality of men, but it hadn't marked their experience at the event. They had simply moved past those men, who made up a minority of the attendees, and connected with the people with whom they had wanted to cuddle. Why, I wondered, had I been so particularly affected by them? I felt unnerved by the cuddle party, and it wasn't just those men. It was how powerful my instinct was to give them what they wanted, as if I didn't have a choice.

In the dream, there is always a man. He wants to get inside. I know that he means me harm, but I cannot let him know that I know this. To do so would provoke him to act in ways against which I will not be able to defend myself. He stands at the door and poses as a deliveryman, a handyman, a man with an acceptable motive for standing at my door. Sometimes my dog, now five years dead, furiously barks at the windows and paces the house's interior. It is my mother's house, dark as a cabin, unremodeled, as it looked during my childhood. I am friendly. I smile. I play dumb. I must not let him in. I must not tell him no.

I have had this dream since I was a girl. I had it after the cuddle party. I had it, mysteriously, every night for most of my twenty-seventh year. I had it last week. Sometimes it isn't my mother's house. Sometimes there is no house. But always, I must evade the man who means me harm. I must not reveal my fear. I must not provoke him.

I have never been a victim of home intrusion. I have never been raped. It is not a reenactment of such a trauma but a preoccupation with the threat of it, with the problem and necessity of refusing without ever saying no.

Near the end of the cuddle party, a man approached Donika and asked if she wanted to cuddle. He explained to her that most of the participants at the cuddle party had rebuffed him. He had thanked them for taking care of themselves. He was sad at the prospect of leaving with his skin hunger still so voracious. My girlfriend felt no obligation to him, but she did feel sympathy. He was desperate, but not entitled. He had come to the place for cuddling and not been cuddled. She did not want to cuddle with him, but she asked herself what sort of touch she would be comfortable with, if any.

"We could sit on that bench and hold hands for a bit," she told him. He agreed, and so they did. "It was nice," she told me afterward.

Donika is the kind of person who fast-forwards to the end of the porn video after her orgasm to make sure that everybody comes. She is deeply empathic and sensitive to others' feelings, but I cannot imagine her ever giving consent to someone with whom she did not want to cuddle. Which is to say that empathy and accommodation are not synonymous. In fact, I suspect that the instinct to subsume one's own desires or comfort for the desires or comfort of another may ultimately inhibit empathy. Donika's impression of the cuddle party was not marked particularly by the desperation of others because she did not feel threatened by their need. She said no easily. Also, she was interested in cuddling. Which is all to say that it wasn't the cuddle party; it was me.

As we continued our conversation over the days that followed, I came to understand that my consenting to cuddling that I did not want had been motivated by not empathy but something else. When the man in the teal onesie had proposed spooning, my *yes* had traveled down some well-worn pathway, sure as a streetcar in its laid track. My body seemed to have recognized the situation as one in which complacency was the only option. Its own interests instantly became secondary to this instinct. As the days passed, I was increasingly shocked by how deftly the mechanisms of accommodation had engaged. My lights had instantly dimmed. I remembered staring at the worn blanket as the man had stroked my arm, my silence as that woman had touched me without asking, the way I'd bargained with the young man for a massage that I did not want.

I told Donika how I'd grimaced like a frightened dog during the role-play, when we'd been *instructed* to say no. What had possessed me to negotiate with that young man, as if I were obligated to strike a deal in the exchange of my body? I knew it wasn't just pity. The world was full of lonely people to whom I owed nothing. Why had the air of annoyance in his voice not deterred me? More importantly, why not my own lack of interest? I was mystified and more than a little unnerved by my response.

"I think we should go back," she said.

I gave her a stricken look.

"I think we should go back so that you can say no to all of them. With the express intention of saying no to all of them."

"Isn't that sort of rude?" I said. "Like going to a nice restaurant and ordering just a glass of water?"

"You don't have to cuddle anyone at a cuddle party, ever," she reminded me. "It seems like part of their mission is to help folks practice this sort of thing."

I agreed that it was a good idea. But what would prevent me from going into the same twilit mode of passivity? After I quit my job as a domme, I had worked hard to recover the feelings I hadn't felt in those dim hours. The body's truth, I'd learned, is indelibly engraved, whether behind a closed door or in a dark place. What happens in the dark still happens, even if you can't see it.

In his book *The Body Keeps the Score,* Bessel van der Kolk explains that "people can recover from trauma only when the brain structures that were knocked out during the original experience are fully online." Anyone who has conducted successful psychotherapy knows from experience that being grounded in the present while revisiting the past is fundamental to its potential for healing, and "opens the possibility of deeply knowing that the terrible events belong in the past." The cuddle party had been not a trauma but a place where some old script had been triggered. If I returned to it, I would be seeking a kind of therapeutic experience, which would require that I be more grounded than I was on the first round. For that, I needed more information. If I wanted to discard that script, I needed to understand when and why it had been written.

"You were possessed by the patriarchy!" said my friend Ada when I explained my experience at the cuddle party. "Remember when I was possessed by the patriarchy?" I did. One afternoon, during a sex date with Tim, a corporate lawyer she regularly slept with, he did not have an orgasm. "I think I'm overstimulated," he had told her, without any angst, and then realized that he had to get back to work. Though Tim had always climaxed during their sex, Ada only did about half the time, which was fine with her. Nonetheless, in this case she was struck by a sudden overwhelming insecurity and panic. He had ridden the train all the way to her home from Midtown, and she had wasted his time! As he dressed to return to his office, she found herself uncontrollably babbling these questions aloud and, to her great dismay, weeping.

"I couldn't stop!" she'd told me. "Somewhere in my brain I still knew that it had nothing to do with me, that he *did* find me attractive and that anyway, who really cared, but still I couldn't stop. It was literally as though I were possessed."

I nodded, now seeing the parallel between our experiences, the way that our psyches had prioritized the needs of men over our own, contrary to our actual beliefs *and* to the reality of our situations.

When Ada told another friend about her episode, the friend had exclaimed, "You had a patriarchy attack! Like a panic attack or a heart attack—but a patriarchy attack."

She shook her head now as we remembered the incident. "Patriarchy colonizes our brains like a virus," she said. It was an apt comparison. Like a virus, patriarchy harms the systems that it infects and relies on replication to survive. It flourishes in those who are not aware of its presence, and sometimes even in those actively working to expel it.

Patriarchy is the house in which we all live. It possesses all of Western culture and industry and has for centuries. But I knew what she meant, the way that a part of one's mind that one has worked hard to expunge of patriarchal values can suddenly regress. Even the most self-actualized women I know have embedded voices in them still faithful to the power structures they have long intellectually condemned. Unbidden, they pipe up: *Don't eat that!*

In the broadest terms, yes, I was possessed by the patriarchy. Still, I had already uninstalled so many of those mechanisms. I no longer hated my body. I loved my big hands and my passionate nature. Never would I suffer a stalker as I had in my early twenties, nor even a creepy gawker on the subway. I didn't even have sex with men anymore, and hadn't for years.

Was I still afraid for my reputation? Did I think that all men were versions of Gus Trenor from *The House of Mirth*, who believed that "the man who pays for the dinner is generally allowed to have a seat at table," and might ruin my life if I rebuffed them? Whatever the mechanism, it seemed pristinely preserved. To understand it, I had to find the version of myself that had adopted it wholesale. Perhaps it could be said more accurately that I was possessed by that younger part of myself. I knew that I couldn't go back to the cuddle party and have a different experience unless I found her first.

It made sense to start with sex work. It was the experience most obviously evoked by the cuddle party. For more than three years, it had been my actual job to override my own desire or lack of desire to accommodate the erotic fantasies of men. It made sense that I would have a powerful aversion to a room full of men who reminded me of those men, that the neural pathways seared during that time would so easily crackle to life and produce their old responses.

But I *had* gone back and performed the emotional retrieval of those lost feelings. I'd written an entire book about it. Those years were also the first in which I'd ever spoken directly about limits and consent. There had been no written code of conduct, but before every session we'd had a forthright conversation with our client about what we would and wouldn't do. There were safe words. However sex work had conditioned me to override my own comfort, it had also given me a vocabulary with which to name my boundaries.

I found myself longing to talk with other former sex workers, so I reached out to some friends.

"Well, sure," said Lara, who is also a writer. "You could technically end a session whenever you wanted, but you weren't expected to. I mean, did you ever?"

Lara is a knockout blonde with a devastating wit who worked as a stripper on and off for most of her twenties. She described once working a golf tournament as a "bikini girl," meant to ride around in the gold carts with the golfers and give them "table dances" out in the blazing sun if they asked for it. "They didn't ask for shit," she told me. "One guy tried to grab my breast and put it in his mouth. I managed to slip out of his grip and ran all the way back to the bus. The other strippers just rolled their eyes at me. They thought I was a moron, because of course I made no money."

When I asked each of my interviewees if they'd ever consented on the job to touching that they didn't want or enjoy, their answers were unanimous.

"Almost every day that I worked," said Molly, another longtime friend I'd first met at the dungeon where we both worked.

"I mean, I never enjoyed sex that I was paid for," said Brynn, a former colleague of mine and mother of two. "But I often wanted it because of the money. And, like anything, sometimes it was more bearable than other times."

"Of course," said Sophie, a Russian immigrant and artist who'd begun stripping in her teens. "But I wasn't inside my own body enough to really hate it."

They were similarly unanimous about the tools with which it had equipped them.

"Working as an escort taught me a lot about negotiating consent," explained Brynn. "And because as an escort I got used to saying up front what I would and wouldn't do for money, I figured out how to say what I would and wouldn't do in private sex situations."

Similarly, Molly said, "I think sex work taught me to negotiate consent, at least in an explicit way. The layer beneath—when I say yes, but perhaps there are unspoken footnotes—is difficult to unpack."

None of their answers gave me new insight into why I'd reacted so powerfully to the predicament of the cuddle party. It wasn't until I asked if they'd ever consented to touch that they didn't want or felt ambivalent about *before* they'd become sex workers that something bloomed in my mind.

"All the time," said Brynn. "I thought that's what I was there for. I had no idea that I had any other worth besides what pleasure I could provide for men and boys . . . I was very confused for a long time about who my body belonged to. So during the years of fifteen to twentyish, if someone wanted my body I tended to give it to them. I didn't want or enjoy sex until I was about fifteen, and at that point I'd been having it for about three years. I didn't even realize girls were supposed to, or could, enjoy sex!"

Molly added, "I think I always had a disconnect between desire for touch and the negotiation of what that touch would mean. I had sex for many reasons, but physical desire was, at that time, rarely one of them."

"On a very basic level I feared not pleasing," explained Sophie.

"I honestly think ambivalence was as good as it ever got for me sexually until I was like twenty-three or so, and I had sex a lot—beginning at age sixteen," said Lara with a shrug.

The stories of these former sex workers, if anything, made a case *against* sex work increasing the likelihood of their consenting to touch they didn't want. I wondered more about the other factors they shared that might have primed them for what I began to think of as "empty" consent. I decided to survey some women who had not ever participated in the sex industry. I designed the survey with my own experience in mind. I offered it to friends and friends of friends. In the end, I looked at thirty responses. Mostly, the respondents were women in their thirties and forties, educated, and middle-class. Half of them identified as white, and half of them as Black, Latinx, Indigenous, or multi-racial. They were, of course, a self-selecting group.

I was not prepared for the experience of reading these surveys. They were often lengthy, detailed accounts—entire lives punctuated by unwanted touch. Many of the women wrote at the end of the survey that they had never articulated the events therein to anyone, sometimes including themselves. *Even if you didn't read this*, they said, *I'd be glad I got to write it.* They hadn't known how much they'd had to say until someone asked. However excoriating the reading experience, I was immediately glad that I had.

I opened the survey by asking if they had ever experienced nonconsensual touch. All of them had, from rape to the groping of strangers in public to creepy hugs from their bosses to "the Quaker rub," as one subject's fellow congregation members privately referred to a common aspect of their hugging tradition.

"From my twenties until my early thirties (when I married), being touched without consent was honestly just part of 'being a woman,'" explained one. "It happened all the time. My job as a woman was to roll my eyes or laugh and move on. I am certain there are many, many incidents I have buried. When the #MeToo movement hit social media, my first thought was 'I can't believe I know so many women who have been assaulted.' But when I did a personal inventory, it was a revelation. I was physically assaulted/touched/manipulated on several occasions every year for nearly two decades."

We know this, don't we? At least how common sexual assault is—about one in four women—but I've not found the research on how often we are touched by men without our consent, from childhood: belly and cheek pinches, shoulder squeezes, hands on thighs, unwelcome hugs, the hand of a passing stranger in a bar grazing our back. Really, one need look no further to understand why a woman would be "very confused about who her body belonged to." Or even why she would consent to being cuddled by a stranger. We are socialized from birth not to reject the hands of others, except in the rare case that they emerge from a suspicious van holding a lollypop. It is perfect training for a lifetime of consenting to touch one doesn't want. It is one thing to yell at a man whispering obscenities outside your window at midnight and another to reject a form of touch you've tolerated since infancy. How do we even learn to recognize it?

"I guess you could say that losing my virginity qualifies as a moment when I consented to [sexual] touching that I felt ambivalent about," said Ella, when I asked if she'd ever given empty consent.

"Hmmm, every time I've had sex? Literally. Every sexual encounter, there has always been an element of ambivalence," said Holly.

"Oh honey, lord yes," said Allison.

Every single one of them had, often for decades, some for their whole lives.

Derek and I were both twelve, our bodies simmering with new hormones. We had known each other since elementary school. Sometimes on the weekends I'd walk over to his house—a small Cape Cod with red trim—and we would kiss on the floor of his bedroom amid the lacrosse pads and video-game controllers. This would never have flown in my own house, but Derek's mother was not so vigilant as mine. His older sister, a senior in high school, had just given birth to her first baby. His older brother, Pat, a junior, was more handsome than

Derek in a cruel sort of way, and though he had never before acknowledged me, I had a crush on him.

One afternoon, as Derek and I shared a bag of chips in his kitchen, Pat arrived home with a handful of friends, one of whom I recognized as the boyfriend of a neighbor of mine. These boys were loud and brash, and it wasn't possible to tease apart the allure and threat of them. When Pat's eyes alit on me for the first time, my mind jittered. I was old enough to recognize that he was showing off for his friends, that they all were, and I felt the careening wildness of that instinct, like a bike with an uncertain wheel. When Pat asked me to step into the bathroom with them, and I saw the look on Derek's face—*Don't*, it said—I couldn't stop. I might have stood on the deck of a departing ship and he the shore.

By twelve, I already knew the threat of being alone with a group of boys. As they circled me, my heart sped and my body twitched. I don't think they had a plan or any particular intention to harm me. They had probably expected me to decline. Now there was a crackling blue energy between them that my presence kindled. I think we all felt its heat, what was suddenly possible. When Pat asked me which one of them I liked best, I did not say him, despite my crush, because there was a hardness that I sensed more palpably in him than in the rest, a curiosity in his own strength and an eagerness to test it. Now that they'd finally seen me, his eyes were flat as an animal's, or maybe as those of a boy who'd caught one.

I named my neighbor's boyfriend, likely out of some instinct that his loyalty to her might offer me some incidental protection. Were the rest relieved or disappointed when they filed out of that dark bathroom? Both, it seemed.

It was different to kiss someone so much larger than me, so unknown to me. He shoved his fingers past the waist of my jeans, then inside me. Then he pushed down on my shoulder, just firmly enough to indicate what he wanted. I demurred as softly as I could, indicating that they were all just outside the door. I came as close to *no* as I could without saying it. To my great relief, he accepted a hand job instead. I don't remember anything about the act or his penis, but I remember the pattern of the hand towel that hung behind him: blue flowers.

I don't remember the embarrassment of exiting that bathroom. I don't remember anything else about that day. What I remember is that I never again met Derek—a friend I had sort of loved—at his house after school. I remember how our close mutual friend, a big gentle boy I adored, said, "Derek told me what happened on Saturday." I will never forget the look on his face—part disgust, part hurt. He never looked at me the same again.

Early in my relationship with Donika, after I'd shared with her some of my first sexual experiences with boys and men, she commented that they sounded somewhat traumatic.

"No," I said quickly. "It was completely consensual."

She made a skeptical noise. "Even when it's technically consensual, if there's a big power differential—"

I shook my head. I knew women who had experienced sexual trauma, and what I had experienced did not compare to what they had survived. I would not even consider it.

Now, looking back at that afternoon, I consider the empty fields of those brain scans, the memory of blue flowers, my disembodied thoughts rising like a balloon to the ceiling of Tiffany's closet, the green glowed stars of leaves above as the boy who spat on me finally kissed me. These, once again, were *events*—not assaults, not victimizations, but not what I would call a healthy sexual experimentation. That is, experiences that separated rather than integrated. I want to say that they were not "normal" experiences, but unfortunately, I think that one of the reasons we have no language to distinguish them is that such experiences are quite normal.

Given how much nonconsensual touch the women I surveyed experienced through their whole lives, I was not surprised to see how often they described empty consenting because they feared something worse. Often they negotiated a lesser act than the one a man wanted. One woman, after being twice digitally penetrated without her consent by a man after a date, said she told him to "slow down again and then thought *I'm going to have to get out of my apartment somehow.* He was big. I was scared. I asked if I could get us glasses of water, we drank them, and then I basically walked out the door and into the street." I might have used that very tactic in one of my recurrent nightmares.

Sarah, a thirty-four-year-old writer, described an incident during a college semester abroad in Paris. After being groped so forcefully by a fellow American student in a cab on the way back to her dorm that she felt almost certain the boy would rape her if she declined, she agreed to go back to his room. "I decided going along with it was far preferable to voicing my opposition and risking his decision to assault me . . . Even the slight chance (and it didn't seem slight) that he wouldn't listen to my 'no' made me want to withhold it. It was my last opportunity to salvage any power, to decide what would happen and what it would mean." Afterward, she told her boyfriend back home that she'd "slept with someone," a telling that "broke his heart and blew up our relationship. I didn't explain how it had happened, the calculations I'd made. I didn't understand them then."

"I would almost say this has always been the reason behind my consenting to unwanted touching," said Rita. "It always felt easier to just do what they wanted me to do, rather than risk losing that fight."

Lara described "one really violent gangster who basically wanted to choke me whenever we had sex. I didn't dare to stand up to him because it would not have broken my way. He would have kicked my ass."

"It was just easier to have sex with them than to explain to them that I didn't want to or to make them angry," said Charlotte.

In the years that followed that incident in the bathroom, I sometimes saw my neighbor's boyfriend. A few years later our social circles overlapped a bit, and we were sometimes at the same parties and a few times in the same car. Each time, I wondered if he remembered. (Of course he did.) Whenever I saw him, I felt deeply embarrassed, not only for myself and what I'd consented to but also somehow for him, because I knew he'd done wrong. Rather, it was that his wrongs—both in pressuring me and in cheating on his girlfriend—somehow embarrassed *me*, as if it were rude of me to even know of it. I certainly never spoke of it to anyone. These are the first words I've ever put to the experience.

Not speaking of a subject can turn it into a secret. Secrets, if initially a source of power to their keepers, often transmute into a source of shame over time. If you act as though a happening is unspeakable, then you begin to think of it as such. A year of threatening phone calls and obscene gestures, for instance. A classmate who spies on you and your girlfriend. The stranger who whispers dirty talk outside your bedroom window. Your hatred of your own body. What is more unspeakable than the terrible? The grotesque? The shameful? One of the dictionary definitions of the word *unspeakable* is "too bad or horrific to express in words."

Here, I see two powerful imperatives that collaborate to encourage empty consent: the need to protect our bodies from the violent retaliation of men and the need to protect the same men from the consequences of their own behavior, usually by assuming personal responsibility. It is our shame, our embarrassment, our duty alone to bear it.

After describing the incident during her semester in Paris, Sarah explained, "There was real shame in making a man feel bad about himself because he'd done something bad. It was somehow embarrassing to all involved, and God forbid." Like me, Sarah consented to acts she did not want in order to avoid a worse trauma. Then she absorbed the consequences of that man's actions—both in her social life and in her own psyche.

In her early twenties, when Jessica Valenti woke up to find the man she was dating on top of her, she knew it was not okay for him to have sex with her while she was passed out drunk. "I don't know if I said *Don't do this*," she writes in her memoir *Sex Object*, "or if I said *That's nice*, or if I said nothing, which seems the likely possibility given my state." The next day, when she woke, still drunk, she said, "You're not supposed to have sex with someone who is passed out," but she made it into a joke, and then "he smiled and promised me he ate me out first."

"I have never called this assault," she explains. "I'm not really sure why. As a feminist writer I've encouraged others to name the thing that happened to them so our stories can be laid bare in a way that is inescapable and impossible to argue with. And I realize, and I realized then, that by definition penetrating someone while they are unconscious—even if you've had sex before with this person—is rape. I just have never wanted to call it that."

Reading her story, I thought of Donika describing my early sexual experiences as traumatic and my resistance to that definition. By contrast, Valenti asserts that her rape "did not have a lasting impact on me, and about that I feel . . . strange." Whereas my experiences *did* have a lasting impact, but did not in my assessment ever qualify as assault, her experience qualified as assault but did not produce the lasting symptoms of trauma. Neither of us want to use those words partly, it seems, because the two are so entwined: *sexual assault* (or rape) and *trauma*.

"I believed in boundaries—could even set boundaries," memoirist Jeannie Vanasco writes in her second book, *Things We Didn't Talk About When I Was a Girl*. "The problem: in the moment, I found it hard to articulate what those boundaries were—because doing so might embarrass the man." Vanasco experienced both what she understood as a technical assault and the longitudinal symptoms of trauma, and still found it hard to hold her perpetrator accountable. She decided to write *Things We Didn't Talk About When I Was a Girl* in part because she wanted "to show what nice guys are capable of." In her early thirties she decided to get in touch with her former best friend, the man who sexually assaulted her when they were both nineteen. They subsequently shared a series of long phone conversations that Vanasco recorded, and sections of which appear verbatim in the memoir.

"I told myself, Don't reassure him—and then I reassured him," she writes. In the first phone call, she tells him, "I want to write about it, but I don't want to write it in a way that would be hurtful to you. That's why I reached out. So that I could explain, so that you would understand my intentions." Afterward Vanasco is shocked at these words, which are both impossible and untrue. It is as if, in his presence—the presence of *his voice* alone—she gets possessed by the same aspect of her that during the assault "didn't stop Mark partly because I didn't want to embarrass him."

It is impossible to read Vanasco's account and not recall my negotiations with men at the cuddle party, my uncontrollably grimacing face, my inability to say no.

During almost every single conversation Vanasco reassures the man who assaulted her, thanks him, apologizes, and minimizes the ongoing effects of the trauma on her. She admits feeling "more concerned about the reader's impressions of [him] than . . . about sharing [her] own memories of the assault." At one point she considers researching sliding-scale therapists in his area and actually calling them to ask if they would consider seeing a perpetrator of sexual assault. Her ongoing frustration with this dynamic is the primary source of tension in the book, and it was equally fascinating and frustrating to me as a reader. Why won't she just stop? I thought, with mounting frustration. Eventually she does, but only after performing exhaustive vivisections of their interactions with the help of her own research, friends, and her therapist.

My recurring dream, then, is a perfect enactment of this dynamic: to protect ourselves, we must protect them, devise a way to avoid ever rejecting them, ever forcing them to confront their own wrongs. Our bodies are often the only currency we have in this effort. It is not a matter of how to avoid compromising ourselves, but how to mitigate that compromise. Our bind is not double, like a Chinese finger trap (the German name for which, *Mädchenfänger*, translates to "girl catcher"); it is more decuple than double, or unquantifiable n-tuple. It radiates in multiple directions, forms a complex web of conflicting instructions and according punishments for failing to follow them.

We shouldn't be sluts, we shouldn't be prudes, we shouldn't say no because they might rape us, because we might embarrass them with our *no* or by holding them responsible for their actions or even by remembering what wrongs they did us. Perhaps the most powerful encouragement for empty consent is that saying no isn't nice. Women friends of mine who identify as feminists convulse with apology when they decline an invitation from a friend, so I suppose it's no wonder that when it comes to sex, as Jenny put it, "It would have made me extremely anxious to set that boundary when it was clearly in conflict with what they wanted. It was less stressful somehow to just do what they wanted."

Here is the distinction between giving empty consent for physical safety and giving it for emotional relief. Jenny describes the latter. That is, it was preferable to tolerate sex she didn't want than to tolerate the displeasure of men. One woman I surveyed described being groped, in her forties, by an elderly man in an adjoining seat at the opera. She said nothing because she didn't want to "make a scene or disturb the performance."

"I felt I was 'supposed to,'" said Kate. "That I shouldn't let men down . . . but also somehow I owed it to society?"

The tinge of astonishment in Kate's articulation of this motive is born of a set of values with which both she and I have been raised: that sex and romance are key aspects of our self-actualization, not our dues to society. These values are a result of late capitalism and relatively recent social movements. Sex and "love" were dues we owed to society for much, much longer than they have been voluntary routes to our own fulfillment.

In ancient Roman weddings, the vows would be taken between the husband and the bride's father. A woman was traded like chattel for her value, for breeding purposes, for an alliance between two families, not ever for her own fulfillment. It wasn't until a thousand years after Christ's birth that a pope decreed that the bride ought to be the one who said, "I do." Still, not until the late eighteenth century were young people, rather than their families, permitted to choose their own spouses.

Western white people often relish their horror at those cultures whose languages do not have a word for rape, or whose laws do not distinguish between rape and adultery, or those who marry their young girls to adult men. They conveniently forget that during the formation of the United States, "Nearly every state legislature enacted laws that shielded husbands from criminal punishment for raping their wives, and sometimes even their girlfriends." Remember, too, that rape was not even a crime if perpetrated by a white man against a woman who wasn't white.

In 1993, North Carolina was the last state to rescind the marital rape exemption—that is, "Conceptually and legally, wives' sexuality and sexual independence bundled within the ambit of property rights conferred to husbands." This standard was derived from British law, articulated in the 1736 treatise by Sir Matthew Hale, in which "Hale proclaimed that a 'husband cannot be guilty of rape' because marriage conveys unconditional consent, whereby wives have entered a binding contract and 'hath given up herself in this kind unto her husband, which she cannot retract.'"

In light of this history, the entire concept of enthusiastic consent is revealed as a radical new idea. The women I surveyed were profoundly burdened, as we all are, by the legacy of this history—barely even in our legal rearview. "Consent wasn't something I was taught about," said Ella. "Boundaries weren't something we discussed in sex ed. I thought that if I let a boy take my pants off, that meant I had consented to whatever he wanted to do when my pants were off."

It's no wonder that I encountered so many descriptions of dissociation or "freezing," my own preferred mechanism for tolerating any kind of touching I did not want and felt obligated to.

"I can say yes when I'm frozen, and it's not a true yes," clarified Diana. "It's not really consensual if I'm not feeling sensual. It's just easier than saying no." Or, as Holly explained, "It's almost like I forget that I exist and that I get to not do things I don't want to do. Now I remember sooner than later it's not true. Maybe one day I'll remember before I forget." If neurologists and psychologists conducted a study of women who had given empty consent, how many symptoms would they identify that we commonly associate with trauma?

Reading these descriptions, I empathized with Kate, who hopes "that if I were ever in a situation akin to what I experienced in middle school that I would unfreeze and just scream 'Fucking stop it, motherfucker!' to the guy and slam a book on his hand or something. Because I don't ever want to freeze up like that again." I wish I could tell her that it would be likely, but after my experience at the cuddle party, I'm not so sure.

For her 2016 book *Girls and Sex*, Peggy Orenstein interviewed over seventy young women between the ages of fifteen and twenty. Her demographic was similar to those I surveyed: most were college-bound or college students, and they were racially diverse, though a majority identified as white. She "specifically wanted to talk to those who felt they had all the options open to them, the ones who had most benefited from women's economic and political progress." That is, her subjects were this latest generation's version of the women I surveyed, at the ages most of them referred to.

"Sometimes," a freshman at a small West Coast college told Orenstein, "a girl will give a guy a blow job at the end of the night because she doesn't want to have sex with him and he expects to be satisfied. So if I want him to leave and I don't want anything to happen . . ." Every part of her statement rings familiar, from the assumption that a young man will expect to be sexually satisfied to that of it being her obligation to the implication that a blow job "isn't anything," or that "anything" might include assault.

In a 2007 study on oral sex among ninth- and tenth-graders, researchers found that the overwhelming majority of young men engaged in oral sex for their own physical pleasure and were twice as likely as girls to report feeling good about themselves after oral sex. Girls, meanwhile, were three times more likely to say that they felt used.

Deborah Tolman at Hunter College, one of the foremost researchers on girls' sexuality, has stated that recently girls have begun answering "questions about how their bodies feel—questions about sexuality or arousal—by describing how they think they look."

Sarah McClelland, who coined the term *intimate justice*, found that among the college students she studied, "women tended to use their *partner's* physical pleasure as a yardstick of *their* satisfaction . . . For men it was the opposite: the measure was their own orgasm."

In light of those units of measurement, it seems generous that women at every age orgasm 29 percent of the time that they have sex with men, while men orgasm three-quarters of the time. In the same way, it seems unlikely that, as a 2002 longitudinal study on adolescent sexuality found, girls were only four times more likely to engage "repeatedly in sexual activities that they disliked."

These younger women have undeniably benefited in myriad ways from women's economic and political progress—the evidence is clear in their educational and professional success, their access to resources and protections. Their relationships to sex, however, seem as troubling as ever. For all the sexual liberation they purport to embody, they seem as far as ever from the truths of their own bodies, their own desires, their sexuality as it exists independent of the perceptions and desires of men.

While reading about these girls measuring their own satisfaction by their partner's pleasure, I was reminded of the two years that I spent in a particularly controlling relationship.

After just a few months of dating that girlfriend, when my friends, family, or therapist asked how I was, I would reliably respond by saying how I perceived my girlfriend's disposition toward me that day, how likely it was that I had upset her in some unforeseen way. It is the shared technique of abusive partners, corporations, cult leaders, despotic governments, and many who benefit from unequal power structures and wish to continue benefiting from them: to convince the disempowered to identify with the needs of the powerful instead of their own.

Here again we meet the problem of diction, its suggestion of definitive boundaries between experiences and conditions, between the self and cultural impositions. When the dynamics of abuse underlie all of heterosexuality's conventions, even consensual interactions share trauma-related effects. A girl can experience or reinforce harmful symptomatic consequences as a result of a sexual experience without having been victimized by her partner, without the experience qualifying as a trauma. I suspect that the task of undoing those abusive dynamics depends upon a more common acknowledgment of these consequences and a vocabulary for talking about them. Without it, terms like *abuse* and *trauma* get overused and misapplied, while other profound forms of psychological affect get overlooked completely.

One night in my early teens, I consented to a half-wanted sexual tumble with an older boy named Matt. As we kissed, he asked me to stroke his hair. When I did, he began to cry, and whispered that I felt simultaneously like his mother, his sister, and his lover. I murmured encouragingly, though inside I felt panicked and desperate to extricate myself. That he imposed the bizarre intimacy of this on me felt more intrusive than any sexual act I might have ambivalently consented to. To be alone in a one-way exchange of intimacy is sometimes a devastatingly lonely place. It has never been expected that a man ask a woman's consent before using her emotionally.

In Catherine Lacey's 2017 novel *The Answers*, a celebrity actor devises a pseudoscientific vanity project called the Girlfriend Experiment (GX), which "assigns the roles fulfilled by a life partner to a team of specialized team members to enact Relational Experiments." The celebrity has an Intimacy Team, an Anger Girlfriend, a Maternal Girlfriend, a Mundane Girlfriend, and an Emotional Girlfriend, each with her highly specified duties. The alleged goal of the GX is "to devise a scientifically proven system for making human pair bonding behavior more perfect and satisfying."

Much of the book follows Mary, the woman hired as the celebrity's Emotional Girlfriend after a rigorous interview process that includes repeating phrases such as "How was your day?" and "I love you" into a camera. Mary suffers from a debilitating and undiagnosed illness, the abatement of which depends on her completion of a series of healing sessions—sessions that, without the generous salary of the GX, she would be unable to afford.

As the Emotional Girlfriend, her duties include "listening to [the celebrity] talk while remaining fully engaged by asking questions, maintaining eye contact, affirming his opinions, and offering limited advice or guidance that may or may not be entertained." Every aspect of her behavior is dictated by the GX handbook, from how often she is expected to text the celebrity to, eventually, how long she should spoon with him before falling asleep in one of the prescribed positions.

Mary's healer continuously asks if she is dating anyone. He expresses concern about what he calls "psychic cords."

"They're fixations," he tells her. "Psychic energy that one person directs toward another, often in a nonconsensual manner.'" He explains that such cords can inhibit the effectiveness of his treatments. Mary denies that she is dating anyone, which is technically true, but omits her work for the GX. Eventually the healer refuses to continue seeing her.

It is, in some ways, a dystopian novel, though while reading it, I had the cynical thought that at least the emotional labors so often required of women in heterosexual relationships were acknowledged as such in the GX. Not only was the work of attending to this man remunerated, but it was also divided by category, a division of labor that seemed fairer and more feasible than expecting one woman to do all of it for free. During fleeting casual sexual encounters, women and girls are expected to place a man's physical and emotional interests above their own, to assume responsibility for ensuring that they are met. But in committed relationships, they are often expected to do this every minute of their lives.

The supposition of contemporary romantic partnerships that my demographic subscribes to is that the work is mutual, shared, as are the rewards of that work. Over the course of my adult life, I have had a number of long-term relationships with both men and women, and in those relationships with men, the work was never mutual. Not even close. In fact, when I was in relationships with men, it felt like I became possessed gradually but inexorably by an increasing amount of domestic and emotional labor—the laundry, the cooking, the cleaning, the initiation of hard conversations—until, in one case, the sum total of the emotional and domestic labor in the relationship was my responsibility.

As a queer woman, I suspect that I have spent less time around men as an adult than most straight women my age, and a lot less time catering to them. Nonetheless, with the hours I have spent listening to men, "while remaining fully engaged by asking questions, maintaining eye contact, affirming [their] opinions, and offering limited advice or guidance that may or may not be entertained," I could have written many more books. If I had been paid for that labor, I would not be concerned about my eventual retirement.

However perverse the premise of the GX, it is built on solid logic, on the idea that a woman cannot simultaneously fulfill all of these forms of labor successfully. It would simply be too exhausting.

I wasn't at all surprised by how many of the women I surveyed regularly gave empty consent to their primary partners. This is a well-known facet of many long-term romantic partnerships. It is not simply the vestige of legally owing sex to our spouses, but a symptom of genuinely caring for our partners and their needs, as well as a route to emotional intimacy.

One woman I surveyed, who has a clinical practice as a psychotherapist, described how the exhaustion of being available to her patients all day affected her interest in intimacy with her partner. "The reality is that I am pretty much never in the mood to be physically close Monday through Friday," she said. "I love my partner, and I am super attracted to him, and I love having sex with him . . . but I feel so spent emotionally, like I have worked so hard to be intimately connected to people while also having boundaries around myself, and I feel done and like I need space and time." She regularly consents to sex despite feeling this way, though in doing so, she often feels "more connected." Though her consent is empty, she explained that, after sex, "I come back to myself and my body. I feel loved and cared for and able to be more alive in myself. Ironically, it probably makes me more alive in my mind as well, and therefore more available to my work."

I think of Mary, how the labor she performs as the Emotional Girlfriend renders her physically unavailable for the healing her body desperately needs. Is it the emotional exhaustion? Or is it the dissociation of performing that labor with someone she does not love, as I did, massaging my client's legs? Likely, it would be both. Regardless, the lesson of the book is clear: we cannot ignore our body's truth and heal its wounds. Attending to the body without an investment in self-prioritization, in *listening* to the self, is like cleaning a wound with one hand while smearing dirt in it with the other.

When I read about Harry Harlow's experiments, I considered the obvious analogy between the rhesus monkeys that he tortured and the touch-deprived humans who were the impetus for the cuddle party. I wonder now if the more apt comparison is between Harlow himself and the people who prioritize their own desires—perhaps even their own curiosity—over the sovereignty and comfort of other bodies. The common denominator seems to be the dehumanization of the subjugated. It seems unlikely that Harlow would have replicated the tortures of these experiments if his subjects were human infants—at least until I consider the ongoing imprisonment and isolation of migrant children, some of whom may never be reunited with their parents by the US government. Isolation and touch deprivation have, of course, long been the purview of colonizers and abusers of all stripes. It is much easier to dominate a body that has learned from infancy that it has no sovereignty.

In the late eighteenth century, English philosopher and social theorist Jeremy Bentham designed the Panopticon, a prison model that features a windowed tower in the center of a circular structure made up of cells. The watchman in the tower can't possibly surveille all of the prisoners all of the time, but the prisoners become conditioned by the ceaseless possibility of being watched. They internalize the eye of the watchman and so learn to discipline their own bodies. In his widely read *Discipline and Punish*, Michel Foucault argues that the development of modern political systems, while increasing certain freedoms, also brings a new system of disciplines that the state enacts upon the bodies of its constituents.

The Panopticon, he claims, has informed much more than the design of modern prisons. Foucault sees corollary disciplinary practices at work in the modern school, army, hospital, factory, and any institutions that serve the state.

"All that is needed," explains Foucault, "is to place a supervisor in a central tower and to shut up in each cell a madman, a patient, a condemned man, a worker, or a schoolboy." The body that does not comply suffers immediate sanctions, and soon the supervisor resides in the minds and bodies of the surveilled. "What was then being formed," writes Foucault, "was a policy of coercions that act upon the body, a calculated manipulation of its elements, its gestures, its behavior . . . It defined how one may have a hold over others' bodies, not only so that they may do what one wishes, but so that they may operate as one wishes . . . Thus, discipline produces subjected and practiced bodies, 'docile' bodies."

The disciplined bodies in Foucault, like the baby in Lacan's "The Mirror Stage," are gendered male and therefore assumed universal. But if a docile body is created vis-à-vis ceaseless performance for an imagined supervisor, then consider, as Judith Butler puts it, how "gender reality is created through sustained social performances." The manner in which we are compelled to perform for the state is not universal. What bodies are more docile, more reflexively policed, than women's? Not even those of children, I suspect.

In her 1988 essay "Foucault, Femininity, and the Modern-ization of Patriarchal Power," Sandra Lee Bartky writes: "In contemporary patriarchal culture, a panoptical male connois-seur resides within the consciousness of most women: they stand perpetually before his gaze and under his judgement. Woman lives her body as seen by another, by an anonymous patriarchal Other." This is yet another description of what film critic Laura Mulvey coined "the male gaze" and what John Berger referred to when describing the dual consciousness of women in *Ways of Seeing* as "the *surveyor* and the *surveyed.*" It is an integral part of the mechanism that induced my own bifurcated self-image at eleven years old, at fourteen, at twenty-three.

The patriarchal Other polices our bodies from birth with the same "micro-physics of power" that Foucault describes in *Discipline and Punish.* The supposition is that female bodies, like prisoners' bodies, are defined by their violation of rule. Instead of criminal, women's bodies are inherently defec-tive, *aesthetically* defective. To the body whose value is judged almost solely on aesthetics, it is a devastating sentence. We are too short, too tall, too fat, too thin, too dark, too stiff, too loose, too solicitous, too yielding, too assertive, too weak, or too strong. Our faces must be disguised and modified with makeup and corsets and clothing. All of our body hair must be removed. Aging, whose wrinkles and gray hair depict men as increasingly powerful, is something we must "reverse" and "fight" by smoothing solutions onto our faces using a circular motion and paying exorbitant prices for elective surgeries. We must show our "good side," protrude our lips, raise our eyebrows, "smize," suck in our cheeks, and tilt our chins down. As I stand in front of the mirror in the women's bathroom at the college where I teach, one in a line of poised faces whose eyes meet those of their reflections, I think: if only Foucault could have seen the astonishing influence of social media, that coup of panoptical technology. Now we are never not posing, never not posting the evidence of our well-disciplined bodies.

I know all of this. I have known it since girlhood. I knew it when I began shaving my legs at eleven years old, the same year that I smuggled secret makeup in my backpack to apply in the middle school bathroom. I have been living and reconciling this bifurcation for most of my life. With great effort I have reconciled it in some areas: the realm of my body, sexual interaction, my intimate relationships. What I have not examined as carefully is how this lifelong discipline has also conditioned my every interaction with men.

What we are taught as a practice of beauty, of femininity, is also a practice of submission. A trans woman friend of mine recently explained to me how the technique for training your voice to sound more feminine has a lot to do "with speaking less or asking more questions or deferring to other people more." We must not exhibit creases in our faces that indicate any critical emotion, because we should not express any critical emotion. Remember: women have been burned to death for as much. We must constantly grimace like cowed dogs, make ourselves ever smaller and more childlike, while dribbling a constant stream of apology. It is not a coincidence that the apex of feminine beauty is nearly identical to that of physical powerlessness.

"Women's typical body language," explains Bartky, "is understood to be the language of subordination when it is enacted by men in male status hierarchies." Indeed, men whose gestures and body language are interpreted as "feminine" know better than anyone how such presentation inspires discipline and domination by other men.

While the disciplining force of the state in a prison or a school or an army is clear—at least in conception—and is enforced by designated prison guards, generals, and teachers, the panoptical agents that coerce women's bodies are largely anonymous. "The absence of formal institutional structure and of authorities invested with the power to carry out institutional directives creates the impression that the production of femininity is either entirely voluntary or natural," writes Bartky. We are *expressing* ourselves with makeup. We like to shave our legs because it makes us *feel* feminine. We dress *for ourselves* and *for other women*. It isn't that these things are never true, or that there aren't plenty of other compelling reasons, only that they exist alongside internalized directives. The call is coming from inside the house. That is, patriarchal coercion is a ghost. A specter that possessed me as a girl and possesses me still, that squeezes a yes out of my mouth when my body tells me no.

In 2014, California was the first state to pass affirmative consent standards for colleges to apply to sexual assault cases. Illinois, New York, and Connecticut followed, and more than twenty others have legislation under consideration. The shared definition of affirmative consent guidelines is strikingly similar to the code of conduct for the cuddle party: consent should be ongoing; should apply to each progressive act; can be rescinded at any time; cannot be given if a person is incapacitated or under coercion, intimidation, or force. The school where I teach employs exactly such an affirmative consent policy for cases of sexual misconduct.

The consensus among those who oppose a "Yes means yes" policy around sexual assault is "That's not how sex happens." When I first read of it, I felt a twinge of the same reaction. Like all of us, I'd been well schooled by capitalism and patriarchy in all the things that sex was, and the conditions of affirmative consent were not among them. Also, because that's *not* how sex happens, especially among young people. It represents a radical departure from how sex happens. The idea is that sex is driven spontaneously by desire. And so it is—by the spontaneous desire of men and boys.

The rules that governed sexual assault before affirmative consent—"No means no" policy—are strikingly similar to those that once governed a woman or girl's consent to marriage. According to the Roman *Digest*, "A daughter who does not openly resist her father's wishes is assumed to have consented." Of course, back then, a woman would have had to openly defy the wishes of her family, her potential groom, indeed her society at large. Sexual consent is no different, according to the women I surveyed.

The more I think about it, the more amazed I am that anyone realistically expects young women to easily say no to anything, least of all the sexual desires of men. If I struggle to say no to a lunch invitation, a work request, any number of less fraught entreaties, when I have some pressing personal reason, how can a teenager be expected to stop a man's hand as it reaches under her clothes? Some do, of course, which seems miraculous.

It would be awkward, detractors of affirmative consent laws cry. As if having sex you don't want is not awkward. As if interrupting a man whose spontaneous desire is prompting him to remove your clothes or penetrate you is not awkward for women who have spent their entire lives being socialized not to upset or disappoint people. The only thing that renders the awkwardness of affirmative consent greater any of these awkwardnesses is that the onus of it does not rest entirely on the shoulders of the most vulnerable.

There is an enormous difference between touch that feels bad and touch that is forced upon us. Still, the psychic mechanisms that deploy to help us tolerate acts to which we have given empty consent are often the same ones used during assault.

I recently read an essay by a woman who'd had an affair with an older man that began when she was in her early twenties and he his forties. It sounded like there had been a great power disparity, though the man had not been her employer nor her professor, nor existed in any role of direct power over her. The relationship had left her feeling used, and probably she had been, though to me it didn't square with the claim of abuse that the essay made.

Patriarchy has trained many of us to pursue those with more power than us. I don't think that a power differential equals abuse, though much abuse includes a power differential. The older man's behavior sounds questionable in a number of ways, but not abusive. There was no coercion, except perhaps that of the panoptical patriarchal culture that had conditioned her. Where we should draw the line between the abusive nature of a patriarchal society and abusive acts by individuals is not always clear. As Ada said, "Patriarchy colonizes our brains like a virus." I do think that detangling concepts of abuse and trauma to identify them as discrete categories and finding words for the in-between events is an important step toward that clarification. Such work allows me to acknowledge the nature of my earliest sexual experiences. It might allow women with experiences like Jessica Valenti's to more easily name their assaults. It is a necessary step in undoing the toxic dynamics that undergird our most intimate physical interactions.

I would like to change the culture. I would not like to punish people for who they are attracted to, unless those people are imperiled by that attraction, or do not have the power to refuse it. I also think that empty consent is harmful, and the legacy of centuries of abuse and oppression. I think the person to whom it is given is often partly responsible. I want everyone to agree that the only sex worth having is that in which all parties' consent is genuine, enthusiastic, and ongoing. I want us all to be attracted to people with whom we can have sex that feels safe and hot and nonexploitative (unless exploitation is your thing).

I do not have a definitive proposal for what should constitute abuse and what should not. More expert people have made this their work. What I do have is a growing certainty about the ways in which I have collaborated in the mistreatment of my own body. What I have is the will and freedom and resources to stop harming myself in the subtle ways that I have been conditioned. If I have learned anything from my study of empty consent, it is that I must turn on the lights and welcome every part of me into the room. If I want my yes to mean yes, there can be no locked doors in the house of me.

As Donika and I drove uptown toward our second cuddle party, a quiet dread accumulated in me, like lightly falling snow. It had been eighteen months since our first trip to the Holistic Loft.

"We can leave anytime we want," she reminded me. I knew that my very dread was a reason to follow through with it—to teach the dreading part of me that she did not have to do anything she did not want.

Again, we ascended the narrow staircase and deposited our shoes in the mass outside the loft. Inside, we made our way to the only clearing left on the soft floor. As we settled in, I fought the urge to cling to Donika, an unusual feeling for me. Though the room was more diverse overall, the particular corner we'd sat in was congested with men. On one side of me sat a young man whose anxiety radiated from him in waves, like heat corrugating the air.

"Hi," he said. "I'm Jack." He had a bright patch of razor burn on his neck, and his face looked clammy. I lifted my hand to offer it to him and then realized that I did not want to shake his hand, so I waved instead. "It's my first time at one of these," he told me. "My friend was supposed to meet me, but they didn't show up."

I smiled at him, but distantly.

"I'm sorry my socks don't match," he went on.

"I don't think it'll be a problem for anyone," I said, glancing down. "You don't have to apologize."

"You're right," he said with a giggle. "I'm probably just showing off because there are so many hot people here."

I suppressed a sudden urge to lurch away from him and crawl across the floor in the opposite direction just as Donika leaned toward my ear and murmured, "Are you doing any unnecessary emotional labor?"

I grimaced at her. If only someone were there to whisper this every hour of my life. A moment later Adam announced that the workshop portion of the cuddle party would soon begin. A young woman found her way to our corner and gingerly sat in the only available clearing. She introduced herself as Emma, and I immediately liked her round, kind face.

"This is so weird," Jack said. "I'm not used to being around this many people. I'm more used to sitting at home and playing video games."

Emma and I nodded. Was that emotional labor? I wondered where to locate the line between sympathy and labor. I knew that they were not mutually exclusive, but also that there was a difference between caring for someone and performing care. How did a person know exactly when genuine expression became emotional labor?

Did I even feel sympathy for Jack? Maybe not. Sympathy, from the Latin *sympathia*, meaning a fellow feeling, implies an emotional connection based in similarity between the sympathizer and her object. I was fairly certain that such a connection did not exist between us. Did I simply pity Jack? The word seems more distant than sympathy, and even the OED acknowledges a touch of contempt in it for the inferiority of the pitied, but it also indicates a sorrow in the pitier that, to my surprise, I could not actually locate in myself. Perhaps I simply recognized him as pitiable. The overwhelming feeling I felt toward Jack was repulsion. I saw that he was sad and found him sad, but abstractly. I did not feel any tenderness toward him and in fact felt a little threatened by the extremity of his piteousness. I also understood, even as it was happening, that the threat I felt from him was a projection. I feared myself, mistrusted my ability to say no. That was why I had come back.

Scraping down to the bone of my response to Jack made me feel ungenerous, but why should it have been my job to care for this man? He was of no connection to me, not to mention sitting in a room full of people more willing to touch him than I was. That seemed the heart of it: that both men and women prioritize the comfort and well-being of men over women's safety, comfort, even the truth of their bodily experience. It is the habit I have been trying to undo in myself, and it has been a life's work.

When the workshop began, Adam led us through the familiar cuddle-party rules. When he got to rule 6, "You are encouraged to change your mind," he clarified that it was okay to try something and decide at any point that it was not working.

"You can simply say, 'I'm done,' or 'This isn't working,'" he told us. As he spoke, I felt my eyes prickle with tears. What a simple and gorgeous idea that was. I thought of myself as a girl and as a younger woman—with all those boys and men and even women who I had never wanted to touch me. I thought of all the women whose stories I now carried in me. What if we had all been taught that we could walk away whenever we wanted? What if we had learned that saying no was a necessary way of taking care of ourselves? I imagined living in a society that acknowledged that fact as the cuddle party did.

As Adam neared the end of the list, I remembered the role-play portion of the workshop. I became obsessed with the prospect of being partnered with Jack. My gaze skittered around the surrounding area, looking for a reason to shift my seat.

I had consciously given my body an invitation and the space to feel what it really wanted and did not want. My body had turned out to have very strong feelings. I thought of all the other times that I'd spent years suppressing a bodily truth, and the force with which those feelings returned when I became willing to receive them. The year of crying after I got sober, and again after I quit smoking. The furious anger after I ended that controlling relationship. Why should I have been surprised? I'd been silencing my body in this minute and exhaustive way for longer than I'd done almost anything. In order to commit that silencing, I had spent most of my life thinking of my body as an instrument, an object connected to my psyche but not integrated with it. My body, I was realizing, was not the box that held myself, it *was* my self.

This realization came like a slow dawning, one that had begun years before, when I was a girl, during those moments when the fog of my learned self-loathing would part and I would fill with love for my body and remorse for my cruelty toward it. It made me think of Harlow's rhesus monkeys again. I considered the way that we treat animals like objects, as if their bodies are empty containers, their instinct to survive rattling like a marble at the bottom. The more we want to exploit a body, the less humanity we allow it. Here I had been believing my own body an object that I could yield to others without harming.

It wasn't enough to "love" my body in the privacy of myself or my primary partnership. Like any kind of love, my self-love needed to manifest as an active practice of care. I had learned this about relationships with lovers, that "love is as love does," but I had not internalized it. A body isn't very well loved by the person who abandons it when its needs conflict with the desires of strangers.

During the role-play, I ended up paired with a man named Bart. Rather than pajamas, he was dressed in lumpy black jeans. Despite the repeated instruction to not use phones in the cuddle-party space, he had been staring at his phone while Adam spoke. When we introduced ourselves, he stammered with nervousness.

"Can I kiss you?" Bart asked, as Adam had instructed us, for the express purpose of practicing saying no.

"No," I said, and felt the way that I softened the word in my mouth, like a cracker I didn't want to make a sound when I crushed it.

"Can I kiss you?" he asked again, to my surprise.

"Uh, no," I said, less gently.

"Pretty please?" he said. If I hadn't been horrified, I might have laughed. His response was so counter to the point of the exercise that I felt I'd been set up to have the most opportunities possible to exercise my new "no" muscles.

At last Bart delivered his scripted line: "Thank you for taking care of yourself."

The final exercise required that we all stand and hug as many people as possible. When I stood, faced with the trunks of their bodies, I felt like I was in a forest of men.

"Can I give you a hug?" asked Jack.

"No, thank you," I said. I cringed inwardly, as I did when scooping the detritus out of the kitchen-sink drain or squashing a bug with my bare hand. Not at Jack, but at the simple act of refusing him. I made a mental note to scrub the "thank you" from my response.

"Thank you for taking care of yourself," he said, and it was almost a question. We both turned a few degrees away from each other.

"Can I hug you?" asked a second man, a third, and a fourth.

"No," I said to all of them, clenching inside each time. When a small man in plaid pajamas I read as gay asked me, I checked inside and found that I wouldn't mind hugging him. Before I could say yes, I became acutely conscious of the fact that we were surrounded by men I'd refused. Surely they would notice if I said yes to him after I'd rebuffed them. I smiled at him, genuinely, and said, "Not right now, thank you."

He smiled back. Even with clearly set intentions and will, it was not so easy to stop taking care of men. Apparently it was even possible for me to set boundaries I *didn't* need, if I thought it would spare the feelings of the men around me. I thought of Jeannie Vanasco's experience during those phone calls with her former friend and rapist: "In the moment, I found it hard to articulate what those boundaries were— because doing so might embarrass the man."

Vanasco chose that experience. She conscientiously set the intention to prioritize her own need for clarity. The entire premise of her book is based on centering her own interests. Still, she found it impossible not to apologize and prioritize the comfort of that man over herself. "I told myself, Don't reassure him—and then I reassured him," she writes.

When I said no to the most persistent of those men at the cuddle party, I watched the quick but transparent digestion of the word move through them, producing flickers of surprise, hurt, disappointment, anger, and a kind of surrender as they finally uttered the phrase "Thank you for taking care of yourself." I understood that I was watching, and enacting, a resocialization beyond my own. Afterward I suggested to Donika that the cuddle party was a kind of incel prevention.

I remembered first reading about the incels, those men radicalized by the combustive combination of their own entitlement, sexual frustration, and misogyny, who believe that women owe them sex. Their complaints and manifestos are easy to find but too sickening to linger over. A few minutes' perusal will answer any questions one might have about whether Elliot Rodgers, who killed six people and injured many more in the 2014 Isla Vista killings, is alone in his violent rage and hatred toward women for refusing him sex. It is an abhorrent set of beliefs but not a mysterious one. Women all over the world have owed men sex for centuries. Belief in the sovereignty of female bodies is far from universal and still so new where adopted that our own minds have yet to catch up. Our culture and thus our minds are riddled with contradictions.

What if boys were socialized as they are at the cuddle party? I wondered. What if Alex, my childhood neighbor, had learned to redirect that route from desire to fear to hate and aggression? *Thank you for taking care of yourself.* From a certain perspective, it would be so easy to change everything. If only we hadn't been spoiled for so long. If only we all wanted to.

"Is there anyone you want to cuddle with?" Donika asked me. I shrugged. Her return experience of the cuddle party seemed markedly different than the first time, and she later confirmed this. "When we came to the first party," she said, "I was really touch-deprived. I had been living in a place where no one hugged, and I was depressed and isolated. I had that skin hunger." That, I understood, was the purpose of the cuddle party. While my own use of it to practice identifying and articulating my boundaries was not inappropriate, it wasn't entirely the point. The air of desperation in some of its attendees that so unsettled me was evidence that they were in exactly the right place.

As we consulted each other, a man approached us. I had declined his invitation to hug during the earlier exercise. We all made easy conversation for a few minutes.

"Can I hug you?" he asked, his gaze shifting from me to Donika.

"Sure," she said with a shrug. He immediately reached his arms around both of us.

"Whoa, hold on a minute," Donika said, raising her hands. "Melissa didn't give her consent."

"Ah, right," he said amenably, though I detected a faint trace of annoyance. "Can I hug you?"

"Okay," I said. He resumed, and during the few moments that he hugged us both, I understood that I had not actually wanted him to. It reminded me of the anxiety I feel whenever I set a boundary with a friend or colleague. If they receive it gracefully or demonstrate their respect for it, I often fight an urge to express my "gratitude" by erasing the boundary. In the moment, agreeing to hug him had felt like the only option. His accommodation had bought him the hug. Here was the mechanism, so deeply embedded, its belief that asserting my body's sovereignty was rude, or a breach of some unspoken contract.

I wandered into the kitchen to gnaw on some baby carrots, and a tall woman with long brown hair joined me. Her name was Brenda, and she had freckles and a steady gaze.

"Would you like to cuddle, Melissa?" she asked.

"Okay," I said. "What kind of cuddling are you interested in?"

"Maybe something like that?" she said, and indicated two people spooning tightly on the floor.

"Hmmm," I said. "Maybe just sitting and hugging?" She agreed, and we located a clearing on the floor and sat. After some adjusting, we found a comfortable arrangement of arms and torsos. I kept scanning myself to see if I was still comfortable. *Are you okay?* I asked. *Is this okay?* It was so easy when I remembered to ask.

There was room for this kind of internal dialogue during my interaction with Brenda as there hadn't been with most of the men I'd encountered. Their needs were expressed offensively; they intruded into the space where my own feelings occurred, scrambled the signals by creating new, reactionary ones.

Boundaries can be an opaque concept; it has so many applications, though it is often quite clear where they exist and where they don't. The capaciousness of my interaction with Brenda told me that she recognized the metaphysical boundary between us. She did not rate her own agency over mine, nor was she interested in manipulating or directing me. Brenda was interested in a mutually consensual interaction. My exchange with her clarified how those men had wanted to reach into my space and prod me toward what they wanted, how they valued my interest less than the touch they sought.

Misogyny filters so granularly into action. Those men did not hate me, as a hungry person does not hate a refrigerator. They simply valued their own needs above mine. And I had seen that flash in their eyes when I refused them, as a hungry person might grow frustrated with a refrigerator that does not open. Probably that was the only method they had been taught. Like the narrator of Cheever's "The Cure," they might have asked me, with the same combination of good manners and disregard for my comfort: "Madame, will you please let me put my hand around your ankle? That's all I want to do, madame."

When we left the loft, and the cold air splashed against my face, I wanted to scream. Not with any particular feeling, but to release the tension of paying such close attention to myself.

In the weeks that followed, I thought of the man who had hugged us near the end of the party with increasing resentment. My own sensitivity amazed me. How many times had I been hugged without permission before then? How often when I preferred not to be hugged? Surely there were thousands. It had happened so often that I didn't even register the minute override of my body's own wishes when that man reached for me at the party. That didn't mean there hadn't been consequences. Now, I was feeling them. What is the effect of ignoring your body's wishes for decades? I suppose that is the premise of this essay, the answer to the question that drove me to write it. Why did I have such a challenging experience at the cuddle party? Because I had so long ignored my body's wishes that they had become illegible to me.

As the days pass, I am increasingly grateful to the cuddle party. The work that these parties are doing and making space for is revolutionary. It has the power to transform the most devastating aspects of our society. I don't think that our society can be transformed without such work. I don't know what else would have prompted me to collect this detailed information about my own comfort, about what kinds of touch felt acceptable and what kinds did not. After decades of not listening, I had to invite my body to tell me. I had to invite other women to tell me. I had to recognize the recurrent experiences that I did not yet have words for. I needed a space where I could say no with explicit support. None of this might have happened if I had not gone there. I suspect that it has been an enormous leap in the quest to care for my own body with the same subtle attention that I have given to others my whole life. I once thought that to realize the importance of this, to *believe* in it, was enough. It never was.

My therapist once told me a story about a woman she knew who had injured her arm. For years, the injured arm caused her chronic pain. It also inhibited her movement. When the woman walked, her able arm would swing, but the injured arm could not. Eventually, she underwent a surgery to repair the damaged arm. After she healed from the surgery, the pain stopped, but the arm still did not move when she walked. It remained stiff at her side. There was nothing the doctor could see wrong with it. One day, while out walking, the woman clasped her arm and thought about all of the suffering it had undergone. She closed her eyes and spoke to her arm. "You can move," she whispered tenderly. When she began walking again, the arm swung easily with each step, as if it had simply been waiting for permission.

If I have learned anything by writing this, it is that consent is a form of communication that happens first within the self. Above all, this is an essay about listening. It was by listening to the truths of other women that I learned how to better listen

to my own. It is by writing this that I learned about the words
we must say to our bodies, how truly we must mean them.

It's too soon, really, for me to know exactly how this will
filter into my daily life, though I trust that it will. When I think
about healing in the abstract, I imagine a closing-up, or a
lifting-up. In my fantasies, healing comes like a plane to pull
me out of the water. Real healing is the opposite of that. It is
an opening. It is dropping down into the lost parts of yourself
to reclaim them. It is slow, and there is no shortcut. Sometimes what I mean by *healing* is *changing*. A lasting, conscientious change in the self is similar to one in society: it requires
consistent tending. It is sometimes painful and often tedious.
We must choose it over and over.

That said, a few days ago I ran into a friend of a friend,
someone toward whom I felt friendly but not familiar. "Hey!"
he said and stepped toward me, his hands open. It wasn't a
hug, but the micro-gesture that precedes one, which I was
expected to reciprocate so that we could move into the next
phase. I smiled, but didn't lean in. "Nice to see you," I said,
and silently thanked myself for taking care of myself.

I reach
my hand
through the water
and touch their
familiar shapes.

LES CALANQUES

I have seen pictures of Cassis, and so am unsurprised though still seduced by its beauty—the narrow winding roads and stucco buildings that lead downward, the shocking turquoise blue of the bay, or the castle-topped cliffs that rise around the nestled port town. No one has told me about the cicadas, though. When my taxi from Marseille stops at my destination and I open the door, I startle at their song. It surges from the trees, blankets everything in its pulsing whir. It sounds machinelike, though I know it is thousands of giant insects, their bodies heaving with desire.

I have come to Cassis for a month, along with ten other artists. I will live alone in a small apartment on the top floor of a building whose tall windows overlook the bay with its green-eyed lighthouse (Fitzgerald finished *The Great Gatsby* not far from here, and it is rumored that its green light was inspired by this one), the cliff of Cap Canaille that changes color with the position of the sun, the town beach crowded with bodies, and the relentless blue Mediterranean that stretches to the horizon where it meets the relentless blue sky.

Every morning I pull open the windows and bathe in the early-morning breeze off the water. I have recently suffered a back spasm whose symptoms cascaded down my body in a manner so painful no medicine could assuage it. While no longer in pain, I have learned something of my body's fragility. At thirty-seven years old, I do not expect it to reverse.

When all of the windows are open, I eat a perfectly ripe peach over the porcelain sink in the tiny kitchen, its juice streaming down my forearm. Then I perform a series of gentle stretches that were not possible eight weeks ago. By the time I finish, the cicadas have risen with the sun, its heat engorging their abdominal membranes enough to produce that sound. I meditate for twenty minutes. My eyes closed, I imagine their thrumming as a ring of light that surrounds the building, each insect body a bright ember.

The call of a male cicada can be heard by a female a mile away, and some are so loud they would cause hearing loss in humans were the insect to sing close enough to the ear. Cicada nymphs drop from the trees in which they hatch and burrow into the ground, often eight feet below the surface. The cicadas in southern France spend almost four years underground, though a brood rises every summer to sing and screw for a few months before they die. All of the souvenir shops in Cassis sell porcelain cicadas, wooden cicadas, tea towels with cicadas printed on them. North American species of cicadas, those of my own childhood, have longer life cycles and often spend seventeen years underground before tunneling their way to the sunlight and climbing out of their old bodies.

It has been seventeen years since my last visit to France, a trip I haven't thought about in a long time, but whose details start returning to me the way the language does. Words emerge from my mouth at the market that I didn't know were buried there—*seulement, les fenêtres, désolée*—jostled loose by the voices around me, risen from wherever they have been sleeping for nearly two decades.

In the summer of 2001, before my final semester of college, I got a job at the New Press, an independent leftist publisher whose list included works by Noam Chomsky, Kimberlé Crenshaw, and Simone de Beauvoir. My job was to sit in the air-conditioned Manhattan loft and, among other light administrative tasks, respond to the novelists who often mailed us their entire printed manuscripts for consideration. "Dear Author," I would type. "The New Press rarely publishes novels and never those by American authors." This fact was immediately obvious if one simply glanced at our catalog. Still, myself an aspiring novelist, I pitied them as I dropped their manuscripts into the recycling bin with a funereal *thunk*.

Most mornings I wandered through the cavernous store-room with its twelve-foot industrial shelves of books and selected one or two to read that day at my desk. If I liked a book especially, I brought it home in my purse. I still have my stolen copy of Studs Terkel's *Working*. It would have been a great job for the person I would have been if I had not been addicted to heroin.

I was only twenty, but already beyond the charmed phase of believing I could outsmart the drug. I had begun trying to stop and still thought I might be able to do so without help. Certainly my boyfriend, who'd been a junkie much longer than me, wasn't offering any. I'd moved to New York two years before, under the mistaken impression that Boston and the boyfriend were my problem. My habit had followed me, and eventually so did he.

When I got my first paycheck from the New Press, he waited with me in the icy lobby of a Fifth Avenue bank to cash it. As the sweat turned cold on our backs, my boyfriend sucked on a free lollipop and tried to convince me to buy dope with the money, to find some cocaine for speedballs. The hard candy rattled against his teeth as he whispered in my ear. Sick of the cloying red smell, I left the teller and tucked the bills into my wallet.

"Stop it!" I hissed. The inside of my arm was still bruised from our last binge, visible even through the makeup I'd smeared there. I already sensed the crawly feeling in my skin that I'd come to recognize as the first sign of withdrawal, but I didn't want to use again. I wanted to spend my paycheck like a normal college student: on a trip or books or my credit card debt. As we pushed through the heavy double doors and stepped onto the steamy sidewalk, I shouted at him. "We're fucking junkies! It's not okay!"

He rolled his eyes and spat the cardboard stick onto the concrete. "Stop being dramatic."

A week later, I quit my job and spent my entire second paycheck —and some supplemental funds from my parents— on a one-way ticket to Paris.

A white yacht draws a line across the blue water like fabric scissors. Two men unload orange sea kayaks from a truck on the shore. I sit in a wooden chair in front of the window and slowly lift my left leg as I tilt my head back. The exercise is called nerve-flossing. I imagine my sciatic nerve—pink and tensile as fishing wire—disentangling from the soft tissue that surrounds it.

As I perform the repetitions, I try to remember the dream that woke me. It was a familiar one, a version of which I have had for twenty years. In it, I am trying to shake that old junkie boyfriend, the one who first gave me heroin. Everywhere I go, there he is like a stray dog with his slumped shoulders and vacant, hungry eyes. *Go away!* I shout at him. In the dream, I am my present-day self, fully aware of how absurd it is that he should appear, wanting to get high with me. The only time I've seen him in the last eighteen years was when he showed up drunk to my first book party. In the dream, every time he appears, I fill with fury and panic. Why won't he go away? Why doesn't he know that he is already gone?

After thirty motions I am ready to scream. Not in pain, but from boredom. The thing they don't tell you about physical therapy is how torturously boring it is. It has never taken me this long to heal from an injury. I haven't had many in my lifetime. Since childhood, I have catapulted through life as if spring-loaded. My knees are smudged with scars, and I still skin them at least a couple of times per year. My ankles roll out of the heels I've worn since my teens, and I fall off bikes as though the ground were magnetized. My body has always snapped back into place like hearty elastic.

When the back spasm had eased after a couple of days, I shook with relief. I made plans with friends, assuming that I'd be fully recovered in a few more days. Then the ache began to move down my leg. One day it hammered my left thigh. The next, my shin. Then my foot. It felt like a burning wire, threaded from the base of my spine, through my buttock, all the way into my big toe. It twisted in me, its frayed end showering hot sparks of pain across my ankle and foot. I could only stand for seven or eight minutes at a time before it became unbearable and I had to lie panting on the floor. It was days and many treatments later before I could walk through the pain.

For twenty years I have been an almost daily runner, have considered it a form of medicine that treats my anxiety. I rarely stretched because stretching was boring, and there weren't any recognizable consequences for not doing so. This has always been my way: to do the thing that feels good, to do it fast and frequently. The doctors told me that this strategy had made me vulnerable to injury. The nine weeks after my spasm were the longest I'd gone without running since I was eighteen years old. I also wasn't able to attend my recovery meetings or enjoy much social interaction. Though the injury didn't prevent me from my daily journaling, meditation, and writing practices, for a while my panic did.

My beloved refers to these activities as my "modules." A few months into our relationship, she observed the set of practices of which I make sure to include two or three in any given day, though my best days include all six: morning journaling, a meeting, exercise, meditation, writing, and meaningful contact with friends. Most of these activities serve other roles in my life and are motivated by multiple intentions, but my emotional balance depends on all of them. The regularity with which I practice each one is a routine of personal maintenance without which I would undergo a personality shift so dramatic that it isn't hyperbole to say that I would be a different person.

"A different person?" she asked, soon after we met.

"A different person," I said.

The only luggage I'd brought to Paris was my backpack. When I landed at the Charles de Gaulle airport at midday, I carried it off the plane, groggy with sleep. The airport teemed with people, a cloud of cigarette smoke wafting over their heads. (Smoking wasn't banned in French airports, hospitals, or schools until 2008.) I pulled a pack of Parliaments out of my pocket and lit one, then followed the signs toward the exit.

I studied French until I dropped out of high school, and then followed it with four more years in college. I had an aptitude and a decent knowledge of grammar and vocabulary, though I'd never tested it among native speakers. Words that I recognized jumped out of passing conversations, but I was surprised by how little I understood. My accent was good, so when I asked for directions, people assumed I spoke fluently and rattled off instructions far faster than I could comprehend them. I nodded, *merci beaucoup*, and continued on, still lost.

Using my Lonely Planet guidebook and the free map of the Paris Metro, I found my way to the first hostel on my list. The drab building was on a residential street, and the young woman at the front desk ignored me until I began speaking. As soon as I struggled for a word, she interrupted me in English. After I'd paid, she led me to a room with bunk beds lining the walls, barracks style. The afternoon light filtered weakly onto the floor from a small barred window. I thanked her and climbed the metal ladder to the bunk that she indicated. I had hardly slept on the plane and was numb with fatigue. The guidebook suggested that I avoid being robbed by paying for one of the lockers in the lobby. I didn't want to waste the francs, so I stuffed my backpack under the pilled blanket between my legs and struggled to find a comfortable position to sleep. There wasn't anyone else in the room.

As the room darkened, I heard people return and settle on the couches in the lobby and listened to their voices laugh and chatter in words I didn't understand. My body ached with exhaustion, but worse, a kind of loneliness that transcended that of a twenty-year-old in a strange country, which can be acute in its own way. I had run away from a set of troubles that had plagued me for years—my addiction, my troubled relationship, and most of all the compulsion to make choices that contradicted what I believed, the person I believed myself to be. Beneath these behaviors lay a chasm of despair and fear more profound than any misery of my body. I had tried to stop and could not. I had isolated myself from everyone who loved me to protect my secrets. My life at that point was a small and lonely place, grooved with the routine of compulsion. The only person who knew the consistency of my days was the person I most wanted to escape.

Here I was, not dope-sick, five thousand miles away from my life. I should have felt free. It is a particularly crushing disappointment to realize, again, that your problem is yourself. I had carried that chasm of darkness across an ocean. It was in me. Maybe, I thought, it *was* me. That is the fear that every addict, every person who hates themselves, shares: the terrible possibility that what torments you, what you loathe in yourself, is the truest part of you—the singed and poisonous center that can never be scraped out.

There was a satisfaction in the way my hurts never manifested outwardly. For years, that fact allowed me to deny my problem. I had gotten good grades in college. I kept jobs. I looked healthy. No matter how many drugs I consumed, how much sleep or sustenance I denied my body, my physical self persisted. Sometimes it felt like a test. How much could my body take? What would prove that I needed help? To pass, every time, was a triumph and a catastrophe. As time progressed, it seemed more and more likely that the only way to fail that test, to free myself, was to die. Sometimes it felt like I was trying.

At twenty I had already reached the foxhole in which I had whispered, *Please, tell me what to do. I will do anything.* No answer came. So I ran. I had no other plan. I had prayed that running wouldn't fail again, but as I lay in that narrow bed, I knew that it had. That it probably always would. Tears silently dripped from the corners of my eyes and down my temples into my hair. I didn't know any other prayers or to whom I should offer them. I longed for my familiar solution, the one from which I was running. What I would have given for what had killed Lily Bart: "the gradual cessation of the inner throb, the soft approach of passiveness, as though an invisible hand made magic passes over her in the darkness."

I had no long history of suicidal thoughts, but back in my Brooklyn bedroom I had a packet of razor blades tucked between my mattress and box spring. I didn't plan to use them, but I found relief in the tangible reminder that there was always one more way out. In that hostel bed, I thought about those small blades, their smooth silver faces and perfect edges. It was a comfort, like searching in the dark of a theater for the red glow of an exit sign.

The date of my flight to Cassis was six weeks after my injury. As it approached, I grew increasingly nervous. It would be an entire day of travel, most of it seated. On the flight, I was that awkward person meandering up and down the aisles, performing stretches by the restrooms, but I arrived without incident.

My first response to my own distress is still the superlative panic of a child. The hardest part of sadness or pain or the surprisingly slow process of healing is almost always my fear that it will never pass. It tells me that I will never fully recover, that this particular experience of discomfort is my new life. The only way to calm this part of me is to gently repeat true statements. *This too shall pass. Feelings are not facts. It will pass more easily if you let yourself feel it.* I've gotten pretty good at self-soothing in the fifteen years since I got clean. Those years have formed a bank of proof that what hurts eventually heals, that everything passes, that I have gathered the resources to survive my own pain.

I am so grateful to have made it to Cassis unscathed, to be here at all, that I spend hours devoted to my neglected modules. The entire first week, all that I accomplish is journaling, meditation, stretches, and my physical therapy exercises, during which I listen to twelve-step podcasts, tearing up at every far-flung stranger's story of recovery.

By the end of the first sweltering week, I have figured out that if I want to spend any active time outside, I have to get up before the sun. I have grown so accustomed to the ceaseless noise of the cicadas that the silence at 6:00 A.M. is startling, spooky. I pull on my running shoes and walk the winding road that leads from our building into Les Calanques, a national park half a mile away.

The calanques themselves, which reach from Cap Canaille in Cassis to Marseille, are a series of inlets between steep limestone cliffs that reach like jagged fingers toward the horizon. In some of their clefts are rock beaches, in some caves, in some just staggering rock faces. The bases of these mini-fjords are often toothed where sections of the limestone were quarried for export until the twentieth century. These calanques are thought to have formed almost six million years ago, when the Strait of Gibraltar closed and the Mediterranean became isolated from the Atlantic. Its water evaporated faster than it could be replenished, and desiccated almost completely. The sea level fell by fifteen hundred meters, and the rivers that flowed into its waters drove canyons into the land to meet it. When the strait reopened, the Atlantic flooded the Mediterranean basin. It filled those canyons and collapsed the weakened land, deepening those clefts and forming the calanques. The saltier quality of the Mediterranean's water is considered a symptom of that time period, known as the Messinian Salinity Crisis.

I taste that salt in the air as I climb the hills toward the park. The ground turns from concrete to a pale compacted limestone, littered with gravel and larger toothy chunks of stone. I cross a wooded parking lot, empty at this hour, and follow a sign for "le Sentier du Petit-Prince." The author of the beloved children's book *The Little Prince*, Antoine de

Saint-Exupéry, died in a plane crash off this coastline on July 31, 1944. Some speculate that when the Little Prince describes his small planet as "the most beautiful and saddest countryside in the world," he is also describing this place.

At the edge of this first and smallest calanque, I look down at a row of pristine white sailboats and out at Cap Canaille, its top warming in the sun to the color of rust. The water at this hour has not yet turned the glamorous turquoise that it gleams all day, but is a deep navy blue, choppier where it leads out toward the Algerian coast. I breathe in that salty breeze and close my eyes, feel my body strong on the edge of that cliff. When I turn back, I break into a jog. Careful to avoid the loose rocks, I pay close attention to my softened muscles and feel the familiar heat of their exertion. I make it all the way back to the sloping road beyond the parking lot. When I slow to a walk, my back is damp with sweat and the cicadas' song rings triumphantly from the trees. Blood hums through my body. I am filled with a joy so exuberant I nearly shout.

It was still dark outside when I woke in the hostel bed. The occupant of a nearby bunk gently snored. I located my bag, wedged against the wall, and found that I was wildly thirsty. I prodded my misery to see if it was still there, and it was, transmitting its hopeless report like a TV left on while I slept.

I carefully peeled the blanket off me and slipped my arms through the backpack's straps. Fearing thieves, I had slept in my shoes. I climbed down the bed's metal ladder, past the sleeping lump of my unknown bunkmate. In the restroom, I gulped water straight from the tap and avoided the mirror. When I left through the unmanned lobby, the door locked behind me.

I had no idea where I was, and it didn't really matter. I walked for an hour, until the streetlamps flicked off and sunlight began to spill down the narrow cobblestone alleys. I'd never seen buildings that looked like these—each corner as elegantly detailed as if it had been carved by hand, which it probably was. The yeasty smell of baking bread wafted from shops with their doors still locked. My mouth watered as my eyes marveled, but as a body won't forget its injury, my mind never forgot its pain. The picturesque scenery felt doused in loneliness. Foreign beauty is of no comfort to the homesick. At its core, maybe every despair is marked by a longing to find a home in oneself.

I stopped at a pay phone, calculating the time back home. It was just past midnight. My mother might be asleep, but she'd still answer the phone. My boyfriend would definitely be up, if he was home. I longed for comfort as the cold long for warmth or the hungry for food: my need was imperative, undistractable. I often had an urge to call my mother when I felt this way, though it rarely helped. Even the fiercest love can't treat what you conceal from it.

I dug into the front pocket of my backpack and withdrew a handful of coins. I had no idea how much it would cost to call the United States, so I pushed them all into the slot. I stared at the keypad. A recorded operator demanded that I dial a number for my call. A call to my mother would only worry her. I could call my boyfriend. He would tell me to come home, which a part of me wanted to hear. I wanted to go home so badly. But with the disappointment of having brought my misery to France so keen in me, I couldn't muster any hope that I might be able to leave it there. There was no one to call. I punched the coin return with my thumb and listened to the money jangle back to me.

I crossed the Seine on a pedestrian bridge and stopped in the middle to look down at the glimmering water. It was gray, like the light, though the air was already warming. I imagined sinking into it, the cool quiet slipping over my mouth and eyes. It was just a fantasy; the water was probably less than a hundred feet below.

By 9:00 A.M., I had reached the Arc de Triomphe. The monument sits at the intersection of twelve avenues that radiate from its center in an asterisk. I stared up at the limestone behemoth, its sculpted pillars that commemorate the victories of Napoleon, who commissioned it in 1806. When I was little and felt overwhelmed by my own feelings, I used to go to the beach and stare out at the Atlantic. Beside it, I felt

286

so small. I was inconsequential and thus free. The ocean didn't care about my feelings, and it would be there after they passed, after my whole life passed. Standing under that hundred-foot arch, I searched for that feeling but found nothing. My problem was not one of perspective, at least not only, and could not be relieved by a shift in scale. I stared down at my travel guide, which assured me that there was a hostel just a few blocks from here that I hoped would be an improvement on the previous night's.

On my way, I stopped at a small grocery to buy a bottle of water. As I approached the counter, the man in front of me turned to leave. For a moment, our eyes met. He was tall and lean, the fabric of his white T-shirt darkened by sweat under his arms. Beads of it gathered in the hollow of his neck, despite the relative cool of the shop. His face was handsome but haunted, and from his eyes hung dark circles and a look that I instantly recognized. The moment passed and he brushed by me, hurried into the street. I had only a few seconds to decide. I abandoned my bottle of water beside the register and followed him out the door.

"Attendez!" I called after him. "Monsieur, attendez s'il vous plait!"

The stranger glanced over his shoulder, and I waved, jogging to catch up to him. I groped in my mind for the right words to ask him what I wanted. "Ah, pouvez-vous en obtenir pour moi aussi?" I asked, hoping it was close enough to *Can you get me some, too?*

He shook his head in confusion or feigned confusion, and walked faster to lose me.

"Attendez!" I pleaded. "I have money!" I dug in my pocket and pulled out a fold of bills.

He stopped and half turned toward me.

"Pour vous, aussi," I promised, holding out the money.

He studied my face. I nodded and held his gaze long enough for him to recognize in me what I had seen in him. Finally, his shoulders dropped and he beckoned. "Allons-y."

My relapse dreams are always the same. I have shot dope, snorted coke, smoked a joint, whatever it is, and then I remember that I am sober. In the dream, I panic. I decide to hide it, to lie, a thing I would never do if I relapsed, but the person in the dream is not me, she is the old me dressed in the trappings of this life. Sometimes it is not drugs I have relapsed on, but an ex-lover or sex work—any of the things I struggled most to let go.

The cicadas are already up when I wake panting, the stiff white sheets twined around my legs. I have slept late enough that the sun is high, the bedroom soupy with heat and my chest wet. I remember where I am and sigh with relief.

At a potluck during our second week in Cassis, I tell another resident—a painter—that I watched a video of a cicada molting.

"It was disgusting," I tell her. "You should definitely watch it." The cicada's body pulsed as if heaving with breath and the new body emerged from the old, soft and green. Within moments its wings filled with fluid, like an inflatable toy, and its new body hardened. The old body still clung to the branch, an immaculate husk. How sad and gorgeous I found it, like an abandoned mansion. What a job to perform! The cicada's nymph body serves underground for years, sleeping in that dark dirt long enough to forget whatever glimpse of the world it saw when it hatched. Finally it digs its way out, clawing the dark like some risen dead, until it breaches the surface, born into that shocking light a second time. Then it is discarded.

The painter and I discuss hiking routes that we have researched in the park and decide to hike to d'En Vau, the farthest calanque reachable on foot. The views from its bluff are astonishing, even in the tiny thumbnail photos online. The beach at its bottom, they say, is exquisite; the hike there from Cassis, grueling. We agree to go on a morning during the following week.

My days have found their routine here. Since that first jog, I have beaten the sun every morning but this one and walked those hills to carefully jog the nearest paths of the park. I have begun to recognize the regulars, just as I do back home in Prospect Park: a woman with blunt bangs who walks her old golden retriever, the shirtless young men who unload the sea kayaks for their rental station, and the older man with the grizzled face and the walking sticks who angrily picks up litter but always nods as I pass.

After my morning constitutional, I do my stretches, my meditation and journaling, and then I write, facing the windows, stopping every hour or so to drink a glass of water and do a physical therapy exercise. At two or three P.M., I eat a lunch of salad with fresh vegetables and strong, salty cheese from the market. Then I work for another hour or so. At peak hours, the temperature regularly reaches ninety-five degrees. By five or six it begins to cool slightly. Almost every day at this time, I put on my bathing suit and walk to the nearby beach.

I often think about all the years during which I expended enormous amounts of energy hating my body, obsessively monitoring my food intake and performing exhaustive exercise regimens. My goal was exactly as prescribed by American culture: to embody a concept of beauty that defied my natural form. I measured much of my worth by my progress toward that goal. What a job that was. Sometimes I would consider the thoughts I might have had if I were not constantly thinking about how to control and manipulate my body. Everywhere I went, men stared at me, tried to talk to me, and commented on my degree of success at this quest. I loathed and craved this attention. I often looked eagerly forward to what I imagined as the sexual invisibility of middle age.

Now I walk slowly to the beach in a pair of rubber water shoes that I bought for ten euros in town. My bathing suit is a one-piece. I have smeared my exposed skin with sunscreen and I wear a cheap straw hat that I bought with the water shoes. I am not wearing waterproof mascara. I have not shaved my armpits or worn antiperspirant in over a year. If my younger self could recognize me, she would be horrified. Or maybe not. Maybe she would feel as relieved as I now do to live in a body that I do not hate and have some idea how to care for. I'm grateful that I didn't even have to wait until middle age, that my sexual visibility to men on the street has decreased in direct proportion to the increase in my own sexual fulfillment.

I leave my towel on the smooth rocks of the beach and make my way into the water. It is cooler than other Mediterranean beaches due to the geologic history of the calanques, but warmer than the waters of the Cape where I grew up. I ease in and swim a slow breaststroke out beyond where the children play, until my feet can no longer reach the bottom. I make my way across the area designated by white buoys threaded with plastic rope, enjoying how the water's cool hands cradle every part of me. I feel the work of my arms, the motion of my powerful thighs, the sun on my flexing back.

I am ambivalent about the hike. I have only my running shoes, no hiking boots, and am wary of my tendency to push my body too far. Extremity holds an allure for me that will likely never wane. I have learned to resist it in so many ways, but I am still learning. On the heels of this painful recent lesson, I am wary of asking my body to do anything touted as "grueling." While a part of me withers at the careful person I'm becoming, another part rejoices. I am finally under the care of someone who is careful with me.

I text my painter friend the day before our hike. "If it doesn't feel safe," I say, "I'll want to just turn back, if that's okay." She agrees and we plan to depart at seven the following morning. That afternoon I fill a backpack with the largest bottle of water that will fit in it. I add a beach towel, sunscreen, granola bars, and grapes that I carefully wash and pack in a resealable plastic bag. I set the pack by the door and go to bed before the cicadas have quieted.

Instead of tiny glassine bags, the French heroin came in a packet of tinfoil. The powder inside wasn't white but brownish, the color of tea water, and we had to snort more of it than I was used to. Once high, we both stopped sweating. We didn't part ways, but that doesn't surprise me. Active addiction is a lonely condition, and it feels good to share your relief with someone. We wandered around the neighborhood to a small park where we sat on a bench and smoked. Ahmed was Algerian, had come to Paris as a teenager with his father. When I asked where his father was now, he just shrugged.

He didn't speak any English, so we spoke in simple French. Because I was high, I didn't hesitate to interrupt and ask him to repeat a word or explain to me what it meant. To do so, he pantomimed, offered synonyms, and often employed additional words that I needed him to explain. I'll never know if he was patient because he was high or because he was patient, but I suspect the latter. Junkies are often sweet-natured people, embroiled in the cycle of dependency precisely because they otherwise feel too permeable for this world. Of all drugs, opiates are the most effective (short-term) treatment for anxiety. *What's the difference between a junkie and an alcoholic?* the joke goes. *They will both steal your wallet, but a junkie will help you look for it.*

He helped me find the second hostel and waited while I checked in. Was it so much better than the first, or was I just high and happy to have made a friend? Ahmed and I agreed to meet the next day at noon.

After we got high that second day, I made him walk to the Eiffel Tower with me, though he rolled his eyes at my request. "I know," I told him. "It's like the Statue of Liberty, in New York. For tourists only." I shrugged. "Je suis une touriste!"

On the way, I bought a bag of licorice and we shared it on a bench in the small park near the tower, gnawing on the candy as we watched more obvious tourists sweat in fanny packs and point their cameras. He had begun correcting my French, which I welcomed.

"Je suis lesbienne," I told him. It was more than half true, but that's not why I said it. We were having such a good time, and a come-on might sour it. I hadn't detected any sleazy vibes from him, and a sated junkie is a pretty safe bet, as far as men are concerned, but I didn't want to take any chances.

"Moi aussi," he said with a shrug, "je suis gay," and rooted around in the paper bag for another coconut-coated licorice, his favorite. I laughed in happy surprise. I hadn't even considered that he might be gay. He didn't emit the familiar signals, but then, I lived in a place where it was relatively safe to do so. I had grown up in a home where it was welcomed. It was possible for me to forget sometimes how rare that was, how many of us must learn how not to reveal ourselves.

When he found his candy, he looked up and smiled at me. His first real smile. Ahmed looked about thirty but could have been anywhere within six or seven years of that. Sometimes, when his eyes began to close and the creases in his face deepened, he looked ancient. His teeth were crooked and yellowed, but that smile transformed his face into a child's. When people expose their innocence like that, I almost have to look away. I can't bear to see all that sweetness, how one glimpse throws into relief all the ways it has been compromised.

He wasn't the only man I spoke to. The men of Paris were interested in talking. They stopped me in the street and commented as I passed. Sometimes they followed me. The men in New York were similar, though I had more practice at rebuffing them. In the evenings, I would often find a rickety table at one of the ubiquitous Parisian cafés and sit with my notebook or a novel. Not one time did a man fail to interrupt me. It seemed that my Americanness tipped them off that I would be easy, or at least more reluctant to tell them no. I did not easily tell them no. After a few minutes of conversation, I'd ask the waiter for my check.

"Stay," they'd say. "Have dinner with me." I'd try to demur. I struggled to draw boundaries with men back home, but it was even harder in Paris. To have so many fewer words felt exponentially more vulnerable. In English, words were my best defense, but in French I could only communicate at the level of a child. I already understood that masculinity was a volatile thing. Rejection could easily turn sexual interest to cruelty. If they were cruel, I might not even have understood them. When they persisted, I'd agree, but explain that I had to return to my hotel first. They would try to accompany me, of course, but I'd dissuade them, promising to rejoin them later.

Then I'd hide in my hostel for the remainder of the evening. Ahmed was the only man whose company interested me. As the days passed, my fear grew that I would run into one of these foiled suitors as we traipsed around the city. I loathed the prospect and often scanned streets as we turned onto them, but felt safer with Ahmed than I did alone.

We fell into a routine. I met him in the mornings near the Arc, and then we'd walk to his cop spot. Mostly I paid, but not always. Then we would wander the city, sometimes until sundown. He took me to Montmarte and the Notre-Dame cathedral, a place that felt so holy I lit a candle and prayed to whatever god resided there that I would soon be done with heroin and that it wouldn't kill me first. I felt closer to that better ending in Paris. Our new friendship dulled the teeth of our pastime, lent it a kind of innocence. Besides, I was only snorting the Parisian dope.

On my sixth day we stood in the Louvre, faced with the *Mona Lisa.*

I shrugged. "Elle est très petite," I observed, with a touch of disappointment.

"Oui," he agreed solemnly. "Mais toi aussi." I couldn't stop giggling after that.

By the end of the first week, I began dreaming in French. Our conversations were no longer so frequently interrupted by my questions or his corrections. It was the perfect way to find fluency: to speak conversationally all day long with someone who didn't speak English and with whom I felt perfectly comfortable.

Other young people cycled through the hostel. It always began the same, with them asking me in French, or whatever their language, if I was Portuguese or Brazilian or Spanish. Walking outside all day in the summer sun had darkened my olive complexion considerably. I felt a tiny surge of pride that I wasn't immediately legible as American. We were the worst tourists—the most entitled and conspicuous, shouting in our own language and commenting rudely on things as though the French found us as unintelligible as we did them. Before going to Paris, I had understood many of the good reasons to hate Americans. While I was there, I saw how many people did and counted myself among them.

When a handsome hostel employee held forth one evening on the grotesqueries of Americans as a few of us lounged in his room, drinking and smoking, I couldn't disagree, though I did dislike him, the way he talked on and on, never letting even the French women redirect the conversation or interrupt his dominance of it. Still, after everyone else had gone to bed I rode on the back of his moped to a bar and later fucked him on his flimsy mattress as the windows grayed with early morning light. I was relieved when he didn't work another shift for the rest of my time there.

I liked some of my fellow travelers—college students or recent grads who seemed to be living the wholesome existence that I longed for and to which I also felt superior. In the mornings, they would hoist their enormous backpacks on and invite me to wherever they were going.

"No, thank you," I always said. "I'm meeting a friend." As they walked away, I sometimes felt a painful twinge, as if I stood on a dark street looking up at a bright window, imagining the warmth of the lives inside.

After climbing a steep dirt path, we descend the first calanque to reach Port Pin, which is named for the Aleppo pine trees that flourish here. In its bay we find a rock beach surrounded by slabs of limestone that make a disheveled but dramatic amphitheater, the clear green water its stage. The descent was rigorous—steep enough that we had to hold onto the chunks of stone that protruded from the ground, crawling like slow spiders down its face. The sun has barely broken over the hills, but I am already slick with sweat. We stop to admire the beach and drink some water.

"Ready?" asks my friend.

"Ready." We continue up another steep incline, toward the top of the third calanque. This path is surrounded by trees so close that their branches almost canopy the trail. Alongside it crowd the sort of tough, spiny flora that can survive in the desertlike climate of the calanques, whose sister terrain are badlands. The plants here have no soil to grow in and must make do with limestone, rooting themselves in its cracks. I spot sarsaparilla and the bright purple petals of terrestrial orchids, their toughness belied by their delicate appearance. We pick our way through a bumpy combination of roots and rocks, great hunks of limestone worn smooth by human feet that gleam like creamy dinosaur bones, half risen from underground. They offer the firmest surface for a foothold but are so smooth there is a danger of slipping. When it happens, I catch myself and gasp, feel the sweat surge from my scalp and neck.

We stop to let a string of men with bright high-tech outfits pass us. I am gratified to see that their faces are also dripping and flushed. I take a couple of minutes to stretch my tightened hamstrings and check in with my piriformis. One of the masseuses who treated me suggested that I might be holding some repressed emotion in the muscle. "You might want to try journaling from its point of view," she said. "See what it might be angry or uptight about." While the younger me would have screamed with laughter at this, and a part of me still wanted to, I took the suggestion. My angry muscle didn't confide much, but I have since developed a habit of personifying it. *How are you doing?* I think to my left butt-muscle. I think she's doing okay, so we continue.

When we reach the top of the trail, it feels like we have earned a view, but there are only more rocks and desert shrubs and a rickety hand-painted sign that points forward to d'En Vau. This is the final stretch before we reach our destination, and our last chance to turn back and save ourselves some of the return journey. My entire body is soaked in sweat now, my muscles buzzing. We gulp more water and then peer over the edge to what comes. Though the sign makes clear that this is the only route to our destination, it looks as though the trail ends where we stand. There is a slope steeper than either of those we've encountered, littered with loose rocks and jagged teeth of limestone. It just looks like the side of a very steep mountain, not a hiking trail.

"I've never been rock climbing," I tell my friend.

"Me neither," she says. The park is a popular site for rock climbers, I will later learn with little surprise. As we grimace down at the perilous slope, a tall blond family crests the previous trail and joins us in looking down. They are all wearing hiking boots—a man and a woman, two children, and a grandmother. The parents descend a few yards and then return, red-faced, shaking their heads and muttering in what sounds like Danish. They all turn back.

"It must be a series of switchbacks, yeah?" I say.

"It can't go straight down," my friend agrees.

"Maybe we could just try it and then come back if it's too scary."

She agrees and we begin to slowly pick our way down, choosing carefully where to place each foot and hand. I offer corrections to my route as she follows me.

Once, I whisper, "What if it never ends?" and she huffs, but we are both too busy to laugh. It feels like we descend that incline for hours. Can I call it fun? It is. The way difficult writing is fun, in its perfect freedom of self-forgetting. For all my meditation, there is nothing like the presence of mind I can maintain when my physical safety requires it. I scrutinize the space before me, holding the fact of my own vulnerability so close. Maybe I have never been so careful. I once heard someone say that there are no "natural disasters"; there are only human disasters. That is, those made by and which happen to us. Nature isn't cruel, but unconcerned with human frailty. I have always found relief in that, but especially now that I am able to better concern myself with my own frailty.

The incline finally graduates into a rocky trail. My arms and legs visibly shake from the effort, and I have to concentrate on my footing in the loose rocks. The trail leads through a dense patch of vegetation, a humming tunnel of leaves. When we emerge from it, we see the beach.

The inlet, sometimes known as the Emerald and the Queen of Creeks, is a glimmering blue avenue of water within two staggering walls of limestone. These are scattered with moss and pines that grow from their crevices and remind me of classic Chinese landscape paintings. As I look up, I remember that the term for "landscape" in Chinese is a combination of the characters for mountain and water. The larger cliff belongs to the En Vau Cape. Its peak is eight hundred meters tall, and called God's Finger. At its underwater base is a cave known as the Hole of the Devil. The shore is a field of rocks, smooth as eggs.

We pick our way down the beach and sit to pull off our shoes and pass the water bottle between us. I eat one of the granola bars. As the rising sun spills light into our inlet, the water begins to glow turquoise. The steep stone walls burn so white it hurts to look at them.

The water is almost completely still, and warmer than the beach where I swim every day. It is so clear that I squint at it. I scoop a handful up to my mouth and taste it. I know that it is seawater, but I've never seen seawater like this before. It is more transparent than any lake I've ever swum in. I ease under the surface, let the water fill my ears and hair, wash all the grit away.

"I want to take you somewhere," Ahmed said on the afternoon of my last day in Paris.

"Ou?"

"C'est une surprise."

We rode the train to a station in the north of the city, where most of the people looked North African. When I asked, he told me that this was where he had lived when he first came to Paris. When I asked more, he smiled and shook his head. He didn't want to elaborate, but I understood that he didn't mind me knowing that it meant something to have brought me there. I wanted to thank him for that, whatever trust it entailed. More than that, I wanted to somehow express to him that I cared where he came from, how he got to be here beside me—my skinny, funny, haunted friend. Sometimes I loved fellow junkies more than any other people in the world. Despite the inherent detachment of addiction, their wounds were so close to the surface. Maybe it was a way of loving myself when that seemed most impossible. Or maybe it was that we could see in each other what no one else could. Ahmed and I couldn't heal each other. We had no good solutions. But we had both found some comfort, and that isn't a small thing to those who would rather die than spend a whole life as they are.

After a lengthy walk, the houses thinned, and I could see the blinking lights of a Ferris wheel.

"Ah!" I shouted. "A fair! I love fairs! Comment dit-on 'fair' en français?"

"Parc d'attraction," he said, smiling. To me, it looked smaller than what I knew of amusement parks, more like a county fair—a small labyrinth of rented rides and game booths in a trampled field, bald dirt patches strewn with hay and cigarette butts.

Together, we screamed with children on the whirling rides, ate sweets, and pointed at people in ridiculous outfits. We shared a cigarette at the top of the Ferris wheel, looking out over the lights of Paris, the distant Eiffel Tower a glowing figurine. It felt strangely romantic, and I suppose it was. As we meandered back through the neighborhood, the noise of the park shifting to the night noises of the street, I wanted to tell him that I loved him, because I did. We were in a kind of love, I think. The kind that two lonely people with similar hearts and the same problem can fall in, that has nothing to do with sex. I didn't, though, because I had no words to explain what kind of love I meant. Maybe I wouldn't have had them in my own language, either.

I hated goodbyes and opted to avoid them whenever possible. When that wasn't possible, I sometimes went strangely blank. Empty of feeling, I would woodenly perform the correct motions, eager to get away from people who I loved and would surely miss. When we reached the metro station where our respective trains parted, that was how I felt. Ahmed didn't want to let me go. He offered to escort me back to the hostel, but I said no. He kept telling jokes and finding reasons for me to wait for the next train. I started to grow impatient. When we finally hugged goodbye, his wiry arms were so fierce around my body that it scared me a little. He let me go fast enough that it was almost a push and walked away quickly without looking back.

I slept the whole flight home to New York and woke up terrified. I knew that within hours I would be dope-sick. I was also unemployed. The only money I had was a pocketful of francs that I needed to exchange and spend on subway tokens to get home. As the train trundled through the dark, I watched flashes of graffitied concrete interrupt my own tired reflection. I felt homesick again, this time for Ahmed and Paris and the way my days there had come after all to feel like a respite from my life in New York, and from myself.

I woke up the next morning and the following morning, and by some miracle, I never got sick. I gave my boyfriend crabs that I must have caught from the pompous hostel employee, but I never got sick. Probably we had just been snorting morphine instead of heroin. It was a lucky accident, but it felt like mercy.

It wasn't over, wouldn't be for four more years. A week after my return, I used again. A month later, the planes crashed into the World Trade Center, and my boyfriend and I watched the second tower fall from our Brooklyn roof. A few months after that, I kicked him out for good.

My time in Paris was a failure by some measure, maybe the most important one: I didn't get clean. I didn't even learn to take better care of myself. It was also a soft spot in an otherwise very hard stretch of living. I don't like to use terms like *self-destructive* when I talk about addiction, mine or anyone else's. Once in a while, I'll give a few dollars to a panhandler who I know is going to spend it on dope. There are days when the next high is the only mercy available to us. Sometimes our best efforts at self-preservation look like a kind of violence.

Ahmed called me once. I tried to return the call, but the number he'd given me was disconnected. He left a message on our tiny answering machine, and I saved it for years, until the machine broke. *Allo? Melissa?* he said. *C'est Ahmed.* I can still hear it perfectly in my mind, like the voice of the past calling to remind me that it was.

The first morning after the hike, I limp around the apartment. My injured parts are quiet, but my other muscles have a lot to say about the climb back to Cassis. We spent an hour at that beach, and then my friend and I climbed partway up the rock face of d'En Vau to look down at the inlet. "What the fuck," I whispered as we stared at the radiant emerald water, its surface flexing like an enormous living jewel. I knew that the photos I took would only frustrate me with their ineptitude. The hike back was faster, but punishing, our eagerness mounting with our bodies' exhaustion as we neared the end.

When we returned that afternoon, I carefully stretched my whole body for an hour. Then I stood in the shower and let the water pound my shoulders as the swirl around the drain turned gray and then clear again. I scrubbed my arms and thighs, kneading the tender places with my thumbs, picturing the weary muscles inside, the textures that bound them to my bones.

By the second morning, I can go for a walk. On the third, I can jog again.

I came here with a list of things to write. But these memories keep returning to me. Instead of writing the things I intended, I write about the last time I was in this country. The more I write, the more I remember. I spend so much time with that younger self, her savage despair and fleeting reliefs, that I start to feel as though she is here with me.

In the moments after waking, when I blink in the quiet, my body still as the tide of dreams recedes, I sense her there, like a language I cannot speak but have not forgotten. She follows me up those hills in the thin morning light and watches as I stretch my body. While I type at my standing desk, she slumps on the couch, flipping through my journal. In the afternoon, she trails me into the kitchen and watches me slice vegetables against my hand with the dull paring knife. As I swim my daily lap across the water, she waits on the shore with the other young women, their bodies soft and unmarked, perhaps hated like hers. I strike a match to light the stove and see her face aglow, the shadows hung beneath her eyes, the shine of her round cheeks. I heat a bowl of soup and read a novel while I eat it, her eyes following mine across the pages.

We are like cicadas, I want to tell her. When we rise from the ground, we shed our old bodies, but we don't forget them. We call the thing we need until it answers. Sometimes, the one who finds us is a surprise. If we are lucky, we don't die. We get to live for a while inside that new life.

At night, we crawl into the bed and let them sing us to sleep. Our bodies curl in identical parentheses, make of the rough white sheet a palimpsest.

Near the end of the month, a group of us hire the captain of a small boat to take us out to the farther calanques. It is a windy day, and out on the water the boat surges up and down. I can't stop looking at the horizon, that perfect line where blue meets blue. We pass d'En Vau and move on to the next calanque, L'Oule, whose cove is beachless and only accessible by boat. Our captain pulls into it and drops anchor. We are surrounded by massive white cliffs. He points at the base, and we look. There is an opening, narrow and triangular, the pale rock on either side smooth as parted thighs. There is a cave, he tells us, and we stare blankly at him until he urges us out of the boat.

The water is warm and clean and has that green feeling to it. The cliffs tower over us and the sea stretches out and down and I feel very small. Floating there, my hands stroking the warm water, I am frightened and elated at the same time—the way I felt climbing down that rock, the way I felt looking out at the ocean as a girl. I think again of that ancient time when the sea was cut off from the ocean, how low she sank, the way the rivers carved canyons to replenish her. I picture the flood of the Atlantic's return, collapsing the weakened ground, carving these caves and then filling them. Such beauty often requires a kind of devastation. Maybe the saddest landscapes are always the most beautiful.

We swim into the dark corridor of stone. Wind slaps the water against its base, and the acoustics turn it into a growl. L'Oule gets its name from the Provençal *oulo*, which means "cauldron," and as we inch through the dark passage, it begins to feel like we are in one. The water roils around the barnacled rock as if it cooks a stew and we are its meat.

Just as my arms begin to tire, the rock canal opens into a vaulted cathedral. Murmuring in wonder, we kick to its far wall, where the rock glitters red, encrusted with what look like tiny gems. When I look back, the setting sun's light streams through the far opening, and it glows like a hot diamond, turns the water achingly blue. I look down at my legs, and they are blue as the sky over Cassis, the blue of a marble or an eye, blue as potion risen up from the center of the earth to cool whatever hot thing burns inside us.

I float on my back in that rock cathedral and listen to the water and the ricocheting voices of my friends. I stare up at the arched stone ceiling as it glistens in the waning light.

A touchstone is a tool against which one can measure the relative value of something, like a text, though the term comes from an older use. It was a stone tablet used for testing the purity of soft metals. With a sample of known purity, for instance, one can test a piece of gold by drawing a line with it on a touchstone. From different alloys will emerge different colors, ones that reveal the relative contents, and thus the value of the unknown sample.

As a young woman I struck myself against everything—other bodies, cities, myself—but I could never make sense of the marks I made on them, or the marks they made on me. A thing of unknown value has no value, and I treated myself as such. I beat against my life as if it could tell me how to stop hurting, until I was black and blue on the inside. The small softnesses I found, however fleeting, were precious. They may have saved my life.

Now, I am so careful. The more I know my own worth, the less I have to fling myself against anything. When I go back, I can see all the marks that girl made so long ago. I reach my hand through the water and touch their familiar shapes.

ACKNOWLEDGMENTS

I owe enormous thanks to many, among them my agent, Ethan Bassoff, without whom this book would not be. Liese Mayer, dream editor—I wish every author the gift of such a patient, warm, brilliant soul to guide their books. Everyone at Bloomsbury, including Grace McNamee, Callie Garnett, Miranda Ottewell, Akshaya Iyer, Katya Mezhibovskaya, Marie Coolman, Nancy Miller, Emily Fishman, and Emily Fisher. Many thanks also to Kathy Daneman and Elaine Trevorrow.

Heartfelt gratitude to all of the people who appear in this book, under their own names or pseudonyms, in words or in spirit. I thank you most truly for your time and your stories. I might not have survived my own girlhood without the stories of others, and I could not have written this book without yours.

Thanks to the publications in which some of these essays first appeared, often in excerpted or very different form: "Thesmophoria" in the *Sewanee Review* and the anthology *What My Mother and I Don't Talk About*; "Intrusions" in *Tin House*; "Kettle Holes" in *Granta*; "Scarification" in *Guernica*; "Les Calanques" in *The Sun*; "The Mirror Test" in *The Paris Review*, and to their editors Adam Ross, Michele Filgate and Karyn Marcus, Thomas Ross, Luke Neima, Raluca Albu, Andrew Snee, and Emily Nemens.

ACKNOWLEDGMENTS

Time and other resources were given to complete this book by the Ragdale Foundation, Vermont Studio Center, the BAU Institute at the Camargo Foundation, and Monmouth University, which granted me a Summer Faculty Fellowship and many other kinds of support during the writing of this book, including that of multiple graduate research assistants and the phenomenal English Department—I owe deep thanks to all.

Forsyth Harmon, friend and collaborator—what fun it was to work with you. Let's keep making things together.

To my pals and mentors and chosen family, among them many early readers and favorite writers (an incomplete list): Caitlin Delohery, Liza Buzytsky, Erin Stark, Shanté Smalls, Jean Okie, May Conley, Margo Steines, Hallie Goodman, Syreeta McFadden, Hossannah Asuncion, Anna deVries, Nadia Bolz-Weber, Elissa Washuta, Jill Jarvis, Emily Anderson, Helen Macdonald, Lydia Conklin, John D'Agata, Amy Gall, Melissa Faliveno, David Adjmi, Domenica Ruta, Lidia Yuknavitch, Jo Ann Beard, Vijay Seshadri, Lacy Johnson, Alex Marzano-Lesnevich, Alena Graedon, Veronica Davidov, Melissa Chadburn, Lynn Melnick, Suleika Jaouad, Tara Westover, Jordan Kisner, Jayson Greene, Scott Frank, Jon Batiste, Leni Zumas, Lance Cleland, Marisa Siegel, Grace Lavery, Danny Lavery, Carmen Maria Machado, Wendy S. Walters, Ariel Levy, Stephanie Danler, Jami Attenberg, Melissa Broder, and all

ACKNOWLEDGMENTS

my fellows in the rooms—I owe you my life, this book, and then some.

My family—how did I get so lucky? You have taught me what love is, and I also happen to like you all so much. I promise someday I'll go back to writing fiction.

Last and most of all, Donika, my best reader and friend, my beloved, you have made me better in so many ways, made a good life complete—I am so grateful to spend it with you.

SOURCES & WORKS CONSULTED

The Mirror Test

Black Women's Blueprint. "An Open Letter from Black Women to the Slutwalk." *Gender & Society* 30, no. 1 (February 2016): 9–13.

Brison, Susan. "An Open Letter from Black Women to SlutWalk Organizers." *HuffPost*, 27 September 2011.

Cohen, Bonnie, and John Shenk, directors. *Audrie & Daisy*. San Francisco: Actual Films, 2016.

Coleman, James S., et al. *The Adolescent Society: The Social Life of the Teenager and Its Impact on Education*. Westport, CT: Greenwood Press, 1981.

Cottom, Tressie McMillan. *Thick and Other Essays*. New York: New Press, 2019.

Crenshaw, Kimberlé. "Demarginalizing the Intersection of Race and Sex: A Black Feminist Critique of Antidiscrimination Doctrine, Feminist Theory and Antiracist Politics," *University of Chicago Legal Forum* 140, no. 1 (1989): 139–67.

Durham, Meenakshi Gigi. *The Lolita Effect*. Overlook Press, 2009.

Friedman, Jaclyn, and Jessica Valenti. *Yes Means Yes!: Visions of Female Sexual Power and a World without Rape*. New York: Seal Press, 2008.

Fuchs, Thomas. "The Phenomenology of Shame, Guilt and the Body in Body Dysmorphic Disorder and Depression." *Journal of Phenomenological Psychology* 33, no. 2 (2002): 223–43.

Gallup, Gordon G. "Chimpanzees: Self-Recognition." *Science* 167, no. 3914 (January 1970): 86–87.

Jones, Malcolm. "The Surprising Roots of the Word 'Slut.'" *Daily Beast*, 21 March 2015.

Lacan, Jacques. "The Mirror Stage as Formative of the I Function as Revealed in Psychoanalytic Experience." In *Écrits: The First Complete Edition in English*, trans. Héloïse Fink and Bruce Fink. New York: W. W. Norton, 2007.

Martinez, Laura. "Don't Call Me 'Mamacita.' I Am Not Your Mommy." NPR, 7 June 2014.

Pachniewska, Amanda. "List of Animals That Have Passed the Mirror Test." *Animal Cognition*, 29 October 2016.

Simpson, J. A., and E. S. C. Weiner. *The Oxford English Dictionary*. Clarendon Press, 1998.

"Slut (n.)." *Online Etymology Dictionary*, comp. Douglas Harper (2001). https://www.etymonline.com/search?q=slut.

Tanenbaum, Leora. *I Am Not a Slut: Slut-Shaming in the Age of the Internet*. New York: HarperCollins, 2015.

———. *Slut!: Growing Up Female with a Bad Reputation*. New York: HarperCollins, 2000.

———. "The Truth about Slut-Shaming." *HuffPost*, 7 December 2017.

Tello, Monique. "Why Are Our Girls Killing Themselves?" *Harvard Health Blog*, 6 August 2016.

Unitarian Universalist Association. "Our Whole Lives: Lifespan Sexuality Education." UUA.org, 7 October 2019.

Weiner, Jonathan. "Darwin at the Zoo." *Scientific American*, 1 December 2006.

White, Emily. *Fast Girls: Teenage Tribes and the Myth of the Slut.* New York: Berkley, 2003.

Williams, Gerhild Scholz, and Sigrid Brauner. "Fearless Wives & Frightened Shrews: The Construction of the Witch in Early Modern Germany." *German Quarterly* 70, no. 1 (1997): 76.

Wyhe, John van, and Peter C. Kjærgaard. "Going the Whole Orang: Darwin, Wallace and the Natural History of Orangutans." *Studies in History and Philosophy of Biological and Biomedical Sciences* 51 (June 2015): 53–63.

Wild America

Lorde, Audre. "Uses of the Erotic: The Erotic as Power." In *Sister Outsider: Essays and Speeches by Audre Lorde*, 53–59. Freedom, CA: Crossing Press, 1984.

Marty Stouffer, dir. *Wild America*. Season 1. Aired 1982 on PBS.

Whitman, Walt. *Leaves of Grass: Selected Poems and Prose.* New York: Doubleday, 1997

Intrusions

Berger, John. *Ways of Seeing.* London: Penguin, 1972.

Brian De Palma, dir. *Body Double.* Sony Pictures Home Entertainment, 1984.

Chan, Heng Choon Oliver, et al. "Single-Victim and Serial Sexual Homicide Offenders: Differences in Crime, Paraphilias and Personality Traits." *Criminal Behaviour and Mental Health* 25, no. 1 (2014): 66–78.

Cheever, John. "The Cure." *The Stories of John Cheever.* New York: Alfred A. Knopf, 1978.

Ellroy, James. "Real L.A. Sleaze and Legends with James Ellroy." By Walter Kirn. YouTube video posted by TheLipTV, 9 January 2013.

Gwartney, Debra. "Seared by a Peeping Tom's Gaze." *New York Times*, 21 July 2012.

Hedren, Tippi. *Tippi: A Memoir.* New York: HarperCollins, 2017.

Hill, A., N. Habermann, W. Berner, and P. Briken. "Psychiatric Disorders in Single and Multiple Sexual Murderers." *Psychopathology* 40 (2007): 22–28.

Hitchcock, Alfred, dir. *Vertigo.* Los Angeles: Paramount Pictures, 1958.

Hopkins, Tiffany, Bradley Green, Patrick Carnes, and Susan Campling. "Varieties of Intrusion: Exhibitionism and Voyeurism." *Sexual Addiction and Compulsivity* 23 (2016): 4–33.

Kanew, Jeff, dir. *Revenge of the Nerds.* 20th Century Fox, 1984.

Massey, Alana. "Sex Workers Are Not a Life Hack for 'Helping' Sexual Predators." *Self*, 15 November 2017.

National Center for Victims of Crime. "Stalking Information." Stalking Resource Center. Washington, DC: National Center for Victims of Crime, 2011.

Penhall, Joe. *Mindhunter.* Denver and Delilah Productions and Panic Pictures (II), 2017.

Thesmophoria

Bernini, Gian Lorenzo. *The Rape of Proserpina*, 1621–22. Marble. Galleria Borghese, Rome.

Carson, Anne. *Eros the Bittersweet.* Champaign, IL: Dalkey Archive Press, 1998.

Rembrandt Harmenszoon van Rijn. *The Rape of Proserpina*, 1632. Oil on wood. Staatliche Museen, Berlin.

Homer. "To Demeter." In *Hesiod, the Homeric Hymns, and Homerica*, trans. Hugh G. Evelyn-White, 289–325. London: William Heinemann, 1920.

Thank You for Taking Care of Yourself

Bartky, Sandra Lee. "Foucault, Femininity, and the Modernization of Patriarchal Power." In *Feminism and Foucault*, edited by Irene Diamond and Lee Quinby. Boston: Northeastern University Press, 1998.

Foucault, Michel. *Discipline and Punish: The Birth of the Prison.* New York: Vintage, 1995.

Goodwin, Michele. "Marital Rape: The Long Arch of Sexual Violence Against Women and Girls." *American Journal of International Law Unbound* 109 (2015): 326–31.

Graff, E. J. "A Brief History of Marriage." *UTNE Reader,* May–June 1999.

Grigoriadis, Vanessa. *Blurred Lines: Rethinking Sex, Power, and Consent on Campus.* New York: Houghton Mifflin Harcourt, 2017.

Johnson, Lacy. "Speak Truth to Power." In *The Reckonings: Essays on Justice for the Twenty-First Century,* 67–92. New York: Scribner, 2019.

Kaestle, Christine Elizabeth. "Sexual Insistence and Disliked Sexual Activities in Young Adulthood: Differences by Gender and Relationship Characteristics." *Perspectives on Sexual and Reproductive Health* 41, no. 1 (2009): 33–39.

Taylor, Keeanga-Yamahtta, et al. *How We Get Free: Black Feminism and the Combahee River Collective.* Chicago: Haymarket, 2017.

Nolan, Dan, and Chris Amico. "Solitary by the Numbers." *Solitary by the Numbers,* 18 April 2017.

Suomi, Stephen J., and Harry F. Harlow. "Social Rehabilitation of Isolate-Reared Monkeys." *Developmental Psychology* 6, no. 3 (1972): 487–96.

Valenti, Jessica. *Sex Object: A Memoir.* New York: Dey Street, 2016.

Van der Kolk, Bessel A. *The Body Keeps the Score: Brain, Mind, and Body in the Healing of Trauma.* New York: Viking, 2014.